The RFU Guide to Coaching Positional Skills

Edited by
Ian Thompson

RUGBY
FOOTBALL
UNION

A&CB

Note
Whilst every effort has been made to ensure that the content of this book is as technically accurate and as sound as possible, neither the author nor the publishers can accept responsibility for any injury or loss sustained as a result of the use of this material.

Published by A&C Black Publishers Ltd
36 Soho Square, London W1D 3QY
www.acblack.com

Copyright © 2010 Rugby Football Union. The RFU Rose is an official trade mark of the Rugby Football Union and is the subject of extensive trade mark registration world wide.

ISBN 978 1 4081 0048 6

All rights reserved. No part of this publication may be reproduced in any form or by any means – graphic, electronic or mechanical, including photocopying, recording, taping or information storage and retrieval systems – without the prior permission in writing of the publishers.

The RFU has asserted its rights under the Copyright, Design and Patents Act, 1988, to be identified as the author of this work.

A CIP catalogue record for this book is available from the British Library.

Acknowledgements
Cover photograph © Getty Images
Inside photographs © Rugby Football Union
Illustrations by Mark Silver
Designed by James Watson
Commissioned by Charlotte Croft
Edited by Kate Turvey

This book is produced using paper that is made from wood grown in managed, sustainable forests. It is natural, renewable and recyclable. The logging and manufacturing processes conform to the environmental regulations of the country of origin.

Typeset in 11pt Goudy Old Style on 14pt leading by Saxon Graphics, Derby

Printed and bound in the UK by Martins the Printers

Disclaimer
Throughout this book we follow the convention of referring to rugby players as 'he', on the understanding that this is being used in a generic sense to include 'she'. We do this solely to avoid the stilted use of 'he or she', which could be tedious for the reader, or the use of the non-gender-specific 'they/them/their', which could be ambiguous.

CONTENTS

Contents	iii
Introduction	vi
Ben's story	vi
How to use this book and get the best from your players	vii

PART ONE POSITIONS

CHAPTER 01 BACK THREE
General	2
Attack and counter-attack	3
Defence	4
Positional variations	6

CHAPTER 02 CENTRE
General	8
Attack	9
Defence	13
Positional variations	14

CHAPTER 03 FLY-HALF
General	16
Attack	18
Defence	19

CHAPTER 04 SCRUM-HALF
General	21
Attack	22
Defence	23

CHAPTER 05 PROP FORWARD
General	25
Scrum	26
Line-out	27

CHAPTER 06 HOOKER
General	29
Scrum	30
Line-out	31

CHAPTER 07 SECOND ROW
General	34
Scrum	35
Line-out	36

CHAPTER 08 BACK ROW
General	38
Scrum	40
Line-out	42

PART TWO PRACTICES

CHAPTER 09 SMALL-SIDED GAMES
Handling	46
Running and evasion	67
Continuity	78
Kicking	87
Tackling	96
Scrum	103
Line-out	112

CHAPTER 10 GAMES FOR UNDERSTANDING   119

Glossary	145
Index	147

CONTRIBUTORS

The RFU Coach Development Team:

Jon Bates	RFU Coach Development Officer
Ian Bletcher	RFU Coach Development Officer
Alan Hubbleday	RFU Coach Development Officer
Nevil Jeffery	RFU Coaching Resources Officer
John Lawn	RFU Coach Development Manager
Tony Robinson	RFU Coach Development Officer
Nick Scott	RFU Coach Development Manager
Gary Townsend	RFU Coach Development Manager
Gavin Williams	RFU Coach Development Officer

INTRODUCTION

By way of introduction to this book please take time to read Ben's story as told by his PE teacher and coach.

BEN'S STORY

'Ben was a lad I taught from the age of 12 to 18. He was a secondary school pupil and I was his head of year; I also had the good fortune to be his PE teacher and the coach of the school team in which Ben played.

When Ben came to the school he had been playing rugby for the local club. He was squat in shape, so obviously a prop, but also had good, all-round rugby ability. Being a teacher, my role was to give every student an opportunity to develop a range of skills required to participate in sport. As a rugby coach, I saw my role as giving the players a wide range of rugby skills, regardless of their position.

Although Ben played prop he was involved in practices that involved handling, passing, running, support, decision-making, rucking, mauling, scrummaging, tackling and line-out. The other players in the team were also given the opportunity to practise this range of skills. He was first choice for every age group at school, including the 1st XV at Under-18 level.

When Ben was 17, I invited him and some other lads to train with the local club side that I was coaching. This was a men's team, and many of the players commented on the excellent handling abilities of the young lads; they were impressed with Ben's handling skills and surprised that a front-row player had such a high skill level.

Obviously, as his coach, I basked in the glory of this as a testimony to my ability to get the best out of players in the development of their all-round skills.

Several years after Ben had left school I met him at a Premiership rugby match. At first I didn't recognise the now tall and lean guy that stood before me. After all the usual pleasantries and catching up, I asked Ben if he was still playing. The answer was negative. As he had played all of his rugby at prop, he had now physically developed to a point where he felt uncomfortable in the front row, and was too light. He had thought about playing in another position, but was not confident enough to do so.

Even though Ben had the ability and understanding to play at senior level, I, as his coach, had neglected to give him the opportunity and encouragement to play elsewhere. He had come to me as a prop, and that is where he played for the six years I coached him. I had looked at the here and now and not the future, and had failed to give him the experience and confidence to play in other positions. As a direct consequence of this I had curtailed his participation in the sport.

I would urge all coaches of young players to give them the opportunity to experience a range of positions, not just in training but also in competitive matches. I would recommend that all players ask for and grab the chance to play elsewhere. When the coach asks who wants to play winger or fullback or back row – put your hand up, give it a go and enjoy the experience. When the coach holds a scrummaging session – ask if you can join in and be taught how to play prop or lock or hooker.'

HOW TO USE THIS BOOK AND GET THE BEST FROM YOUR PLAYERS

The practices in this book will help younger players to understand the roles and skills required to play different positions in the game of rugby. It is also a reference for coaches and recommends a number of coaching games based on the development of core and unit skills.

In part I of this book we look at the roles, responsibilities and characteristics of 'units' in the team, such as the back three (wingers and fullback) or the back row (flankers and number 8). The book is written in this way, as players in these units tend to operate together, as well as support each other, to gain advantage in the game. Because of this, these players are likely to have the same core skill requirements, and their development follows common themes.

Each chapter is further divided into sections that follow a common format:

1. General description of the role of the unit and players, their skills and physical needs, such as strength, speed or agility.

2. Role of the unit and players in attack, defence and any set plays, such as a line-out or scrum.

3. Recommended small-sided games and games for understanding, to develop core skills through game-related practices. These games are referenced by numbers that link to full descriptions of the practices in the corresponding chapters in part II of this book.

4. Any positional variations within the units.

Part II of this book is dedicated to details of the small-sided games and other games for understanding that have been recommended in part I.

Coaching best practice promotes greater use of conditioned and small-sided games to improve a player's techniques and skills. The added benefit of coaching through games is that, at the same time, players develop tactical awareness and tend to be more motivated by the competitive and fun elements of the activity.

SMALL-SIDED GAMES

In this book 'small-sided games' refers to games for up to six players. Many of these games can be tailored to serve as warm-up activities, or adapted into general fun games that can be played in the garden or park with friends to further encourage players to develop their own skills.

However, where games have safety or contact implications, such as scrums or tackles, these must be monitored and supervised by a qualified and experienced coach. In this book, for activities where this applies, the exercises are clearly marked and must be supervised by a qualified coach.

GAMES FOR UNDERSTANDING

These are games for larger numbers of participants and are designed to highlight specific tactical elements in the game, such as defensive patterns or exploiting back-line space. In these games players are put into game-related situations, and coaches should encourage their players to experiment and explore alternative ways of gaining advantage from each situation. Generally, there is no right or wrong way to play these games but, coached in this way, players develop their own tactics and routines, which are easily transferred from the training ground to match day.

Games for understanding need more structure and organisation and should be planned and delivered under the direction of a qualified coach. Coaches should encourage players to relate their actions and tactics to the 'principles of play' as discussed below. This will not only help players to understand their decisions but will also provide a general framework for playing in the broader game.

PRINCIPLES OF PLAY

All play in rugby, both in attack and defence, can be thought of as combinations of six general 'principles of play':

1. Contesting possession
   Having possession is the single most important player condition of the game. Without possession of the ball it is impossible to attack in the game, to score points or ultimately to win.

2. Going forwards
   Going forwards towards the opponents' try line is the principal objective of the game of rugby. In attack, going forwards with the ball increases the likelihood of scoring points, disrupting defences or creating space. In defence, going forwards denies the attacking team time and space, and increases the likelihood of them making a mistake.

3. Support
   In attack, support players provide options to pass the ball, to change the point or direction of the attack, or to secure and keep the ball available in contact. In defence, players support each other in defensive units. For example, a back-row player may provide defensive support to a fly-half or centre against an opposing team's midfield attack.

4. Continuity
   Continuity is a measure of how well or otherwise a team plays without stoppage. In attack, this means keeping the ball available through multiple phases of play without mistakes. In defence, it is a measure of how well the team coordinates and realigns its defence, or switches from defence to attack when the ball is turned over.

5. Pressure
   The aim of both sides is to put opponents under pressure. In attack, pressure is a factor in breaking down defences and creating scoring opportunities. In defence, sustained pressure is a major factor in forcing mistakes and gaining possession of the ball.

6. Communication
   Communication is central to all the other principles of play. Undoubtedly, communication is the single most important factor for all successful teams. Organisation within the team can only be achieved through effective communication.

WARM-UPS

Every training or pre-match activity should begin with a warm-up designed to mentally and physically prepare the player for exertion. The principal aim of the warm-up is to increase the heart rate and prepare muscles for exercise in a controlled and progressive manner. However, the warm-up can fulfil other functions: by linking it to the main activity it can provide an opportunity to begin to coach elements of the session. When tailoring a warm-up, first consider the content of the main session and work backwards to design each of the warm-up stages.

Key factors include:

- Always include a warm-up before every session

- Within the warm-up include dynamic stretching to prepare muscles for activity

- Warm-up activities should be game-relevant and session-specific – for example, preparation for contact should include ball carrying (game-related), wrestling (physical condition) and competition (mental preparation)

- Warm-up sessions should generally use simple activities that progress from low intensity to high intensity

- The warm-up should not be seen as a separate event but as the foundation to the main session and supporting the theme of that session.

Warm-up practices

Note: The numbers refer to the corresponding practice games in part II.
Small-sided games:
Handling (1, 2, 8), Running and evasion (12, 13), Tackling (26)
Games for understanding:
37

PREPARING FOR EXERCISE

It is not the aim of this book to go into depth regarding the nutritional needs of players: the reader is directed to look at any of the many excellent sources of information on this subject. However, there are a number of simple 'golden rules' that should be followed during training and on match days:

1. Before exercise

- Eat your last main meal around 3–4 hours prior to exercise.

- Snack after this period, but on foods that break down quickly, e.g. soft fruits.

- Be well hydrated before training or a game. Start taking small amounts of water at regular intervals up to 6 hours before kick-off.

2. During exercise

- During exercise or during the game, take regular drink breaks, or when there is a stoppage in play always have at least a mouthful of water.

3. After exercise

- After exercise your body is ready for food to make up for lost energy and to aid recovery. You should plan to eat a balanced meal after exercise or a game; try to include both carbohydrate and protein at this time, such as boiled chicken or fish (lean protein) with a carbohydrate-rich food such as pasta, potatoes or rice. Also include fruits or yoghurts with your meal. Drink plenty of water to rehydrate. A general rule is you should drink the same weight in water as the body weight you lose during training or the game. Initially it is good practice to weigh yourself before and after exercise until you become familiar with how much liquid you need to take after exercise. Remember you will need to drink more on a hot day.

Key to Diagrams

```
- - - - - - - - - - - - - ->    Direction of pass

———————————>                    Direction of moving player

△   △   △                       Cones

- - - - - - - - - - - - -       Imaginary line dividing pitch

⬤                               Attacking player

⬤                               Defending player
```

PART ONE

POSITIONS

CHAPTER 01
BACK THREE

GENERAL
The two wingers and fullback work closely as a mini-team within the team, sharing and switching roles to provide cover across the field both in attack and defence. To do this, the three players must be able to read the game, understand each other's role and communicate well as a unit. To be effective in both attack and defence, the wingers and fullback must have a full range of attacking and defensive skills: genuine pace, excellent handling and evasive skills, and determination to take on and defeat opponents in one-on-one competition.

ATTACK AND COUNTER-ATTACK

In attack, the wingers and fullback act as 'finishers' by scoring tries. They should have a combination of pace, strength and agility and are often the quickest players on the field. To make use of these strengths, many attacking plays aim to put a winger or fullback into space. For example, the play shown in the figure below has the right winger and fullback coming into the line to create a potential attacking overlap and put the left winger (No. 11) into space, with a clear run for the line.

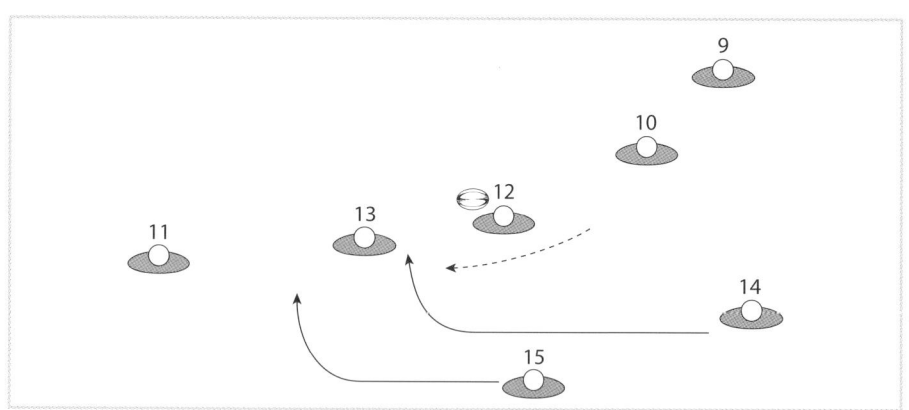

Against opposition kicks, the wingers and fullback operate as a unit to provide across-the-pitch cover defence against kicks to midfield or wide kicks towards the touchline. The fullback and both wingers must be safe and secure at catching the ball and effective at launching a counter-attack, kicking or standing strong in contact and waiting for support to arrive.

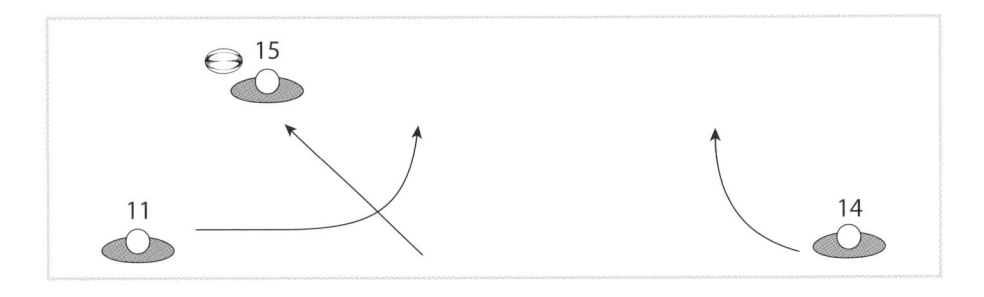

Often some of the most exciting forms of attack are where a side chooses to launch a counter-attack on receipt of an opponent's kick. Because of the positioning of the back three, it is often the wingers or fullback who starts the counter-attack and has space to accelerate and challenge the opposition at top speed. The back three should regularly practise their counter-attack skills from different areas on the field. For example, in this counter-attack play shown above, the fullback has received a kick 'midfield' and decided to launch a counter-attack. The left-hand winger (No. 11) has moved quickly infield to change the angle of the attack, and the right winger (No. 14) has read the situation and moved infield to take a pass and change the point of attack.

Attack pressure practices

Note: The numbers refer to the corresponding practice games in part II.
Small-sided games:
Handling (1–10), Running and evasion (all), Continuity (all)
Games for understanding:
38, 39, 41, 42, 43

DEFENCE

To fulfil their defensive roles, the fullback and wingers must have good vision to read the game and great communication and organisational skills to maintain defensive cover across the pitch; they must also be courageous and technically excellent in the tackle.

In general play, the back three give depth to the defence, operating behind the main defensive line to limit the opponents' attacking options. As the attacking side moves the ball, the back three position themselves to anticipate kicks and they cover for players breaking through the main defensive line or against wide running attacks. For example, the defensive alignment in the figure below shows the open-side winger (No. 14) in position behind the main defensive line to defend the cross-field kick. The fullback (No. 15) is in position to cover a centre-field kick or to move quickly to support either winger, should the ball be directed wide.

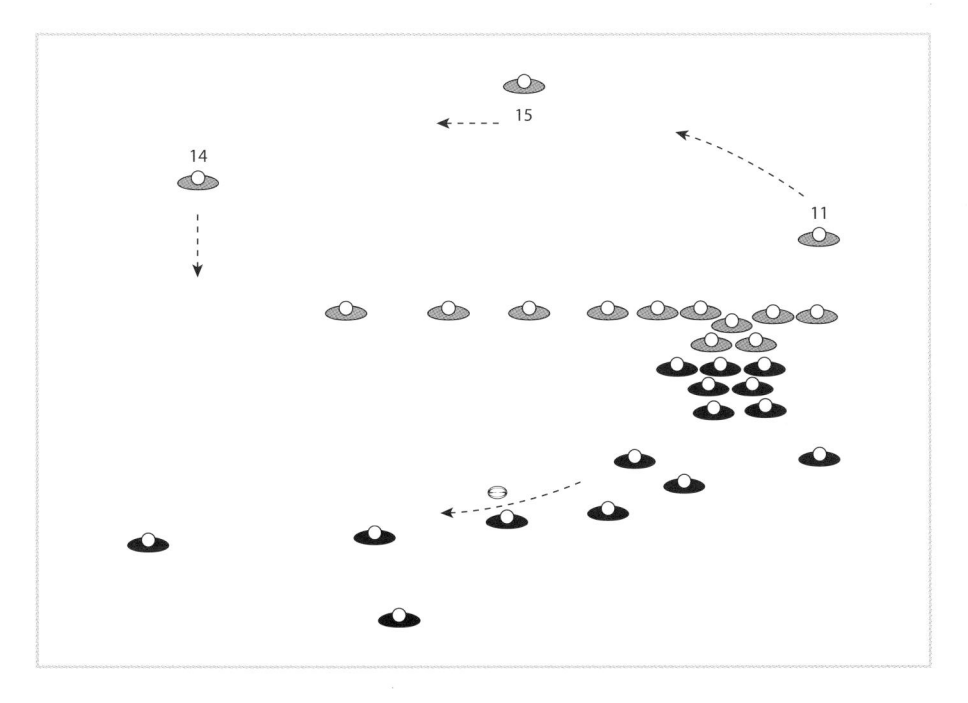

As the attacking play moves across the field, the defensive back three (No. 11, No. 14 and No. 15) move as a unit to keep the defensive cover. The open-side winger (No. 14) moves forwards into a tackling position, the fullback tracks across to provide cover against the 'kick through' or line-break at the point of play. At the same time the blind-side winger (No. 11) moves infield to cover the ground left by the fullback and give midfield cover against a kick back into this area.

The effectiveness of this defence strategy relies on the ability of the back three to read the game, communicate their intentions and move quickly as a unit in response to the attack.

Defence pressure practices
Small-sided games:
Tackling (all)
Games for understanding:
37, 44, 46, 47, 50

POSITIONAL VARIATIONS

FULLBACK (NO. 15)
The fullback can be the most effective attacking player on the field, with time and space to capitalise on attacking opportunities. From a position at the back, No. 15 has a good view of play and must have the ability to see space and identify opportunities to attack. Having identified an opportunity, the fullback must have the pace and attacking skills, together with handling and evasion abilities, to exploit the chance and score the try.

The fullback is central in the back three and is the primary player to deal with opponents' kicks. A core skill of the fullback is to demonstrate a safe pair of hands against all forms of kick: the high ball, the kick through and the rolling ball. The fullback is also one of the strongest and most effective kickers in the team, able to kick with either foot, using spiral kicks for distance and end-over-end kicks for accuracy.

Fearless in tackles, the fullback carries out a high proportion of tackles against high speed runners following a line-break or overlap. The fullback must practise open-field tackling from the front and tackling at speed from the side and the rear.

The fullback is also pivotal in communicating defensive alignment and movement to both wingers. In the central position, the fullback has the best field of vision to read the game and to communicate with both wingers.

LEFT WINGER (NO. 11)
Although players train to eliminate weaknesses, it is also true that most of them find it easier to pass the ball from right to left. As a consequence, attacking moves running from right to left are often executed more quickly and effectively. Therefore, the left winger is often put into good attacking positions with plenty of space more frequently than the right winger. Of the two wingers, the left winger should be the more highly skilled and capable of making the most of these opportunities.

RIGHT WINGER (NO. 14)

The core skills of both wingers are generally the same: speed, handling, tackling and evasion. However, there is one attacking option more often played through the right winger than the left one. Back-row moves are more usually run to the right of the scrummage due to defensive weaknesses on that side. From attacking scrums on the right-hand side of the field, the right winger is often given the opportunity to attack the blind side with a potential overlap. The right winger, working with the back row and scrum-half, should practise attacking in this narrow channel.

Kicking pressure practices

Small-sided games:
Kicking (all)
Games for understanding:
48

CHAPTER 02
CENTRE

GENERAL

Centres come in many shapes and sizes and all are effective in their own way. Some centres have the ability to glide past defenders, while others use power and dynamics to create or drive through gaps in the opposition defence. Some release players into space with perfectly timed and weighted passes, while others use their athleticism to attract defenders and then offload into space.

Although centres may have different preferred methods of attack, they must have a full range of well-developed core skills. These are the skills needed to receive and throw a pass, evade or take contact, accelerate and have good top-end pace, and be effective in the tackle. All centres will be called on to perform each of these skills several times during a game, and to be fully effective it is vital that time is spent practising and perfecting them.

ATTACK

HANDLING

A centre must have the ability to quickly and effectively catch and pass the ball to a teammate in a better position to attack. This transfer must be made quickly so the opposition does not have time to advance on the receiver, and accurately so the receiver does not have to slow down or reach for the ball, again allowing defenders to put pressure on the movement.

A centre must practise the core handling skills needed to deliver a range of passes appropriate to the position of the receiver. A given situation may require a short sympathetic pop pass to a close runner looking to penetrate the defence, or a longer pass to provide width to the attack to outflank defenders.

Key factors in passing:

- When receiving, have hands at shoulder level and towards the passer to provide a target.

- Watch the ball – reach, catch and control it away from the chest.

- Once the ball is in hand, quickly scan the opposition defence for an attacking opportunity.

- If the pass is the best attacking option, turn head quickly and fix eyes on the new target.

- The right arm provides the power and the left hand provides direction, if passing to the left, and vice versa, if passing to the right.

- During the pass, the elbow of the 'power' arm should be kept high to improve the accuracy and length of pass.

- Move the ball across the body, without letting it drop below hip level.

- Practise passes of different length and weight to both sides to improve accuracy and length of pass.

RUNNING AND EVASION

Many times a centre will receive the ball with space between him and the opposition. This presents the centre with an opportunity to challenge and evade the defence. Generally, the centre's attacking line is aimed at the inside shoulder of the opponent, that is the shoulder closest to where the ball has come from. This helps to keep the attacking line straight and also keeps space on the outside for others in the attacking line to exploit.

A centre may try to use the space outside the defender but, unless he has the pace and acceleration to get beyond the opposition, the advantage is usually with the defender.

Key running skills for a centre:

- Identify space before catching the ball and get on the running line into that space before receipt of the ball.

- Always carry the ball in two hands – the defender will then see that passing either side is an attacking option.

- Stay balanced so that the defender may be beaten on the inside or outside by stepping off either foot.

- Effective changes of direction only happen with balanced running – shorten the stride before attempting to sidestep and swerve.

CONTACT

Although a centre should always be seeking to run with the ball into space, contact with a defender is often unavoidable in congested areas against an organised defence. When this happens, it is essential to keep possession, and that play is continued in as positive a way as possible.

Key points in contact:

- As contact becomes inevitable, the centre should strive to dominate that contact. This usually means stepping to the left or right of the defender, and not running straight at them (which would allow the defender to make a more powerful tackle).

- Keep the ball in two hands.

- If possible, free the arms and look to offload to a support runner in space.

- If no runner is available, stay on the feet as long as possible to 'fight the ground' so that you keep moving forwards and provide a focus for support.

- Turn the shoulder to push the ball back towards supporting players – if possible keep driving forwards by taking small steps to keep the defenders retreating.

- If floor contact is unavoidable, control the ball in contact with the ground, then push back towards supporting players.

Very often, the centre will be the first support player arriving when a teammate has been tackled. This may happen in relatively isolated positions on the pitch at a time when quick release of the ball could create an exciting opportunity for the attacking side or, alternatively, a turnover could have serious consequences. It is important that the support and general contact skills of the centre are as developed as those of a back-row forward, and the same practices should be repeated to perfect their contact skills.

KICKING

Although the majority of the kicking duties will rest with the scrum-halves and fly-halves, centres that also kick add to the range of options for the team and it is important that time is spent practising this skill.

Occasionally, a centre may be the player to make a clearing kick or 'punt kick' when the team is under pressure or the scrum-half and fly-half are 'tied up' in a ruck or maul. Another clearing kick from a centre is commonly known as a 'wiper kick'. This is a variation clearing kick to the open side (rather than the usual clearing kick to the nearer touchline) and is usually designed to land in space, still in play. A selection of kicking practices are included in part II of this book.

Having an eye for undefended space is a key asset for a centre. Often that space is just behind the defensive line as they rush up to tackle the centre. To exploit that space, a centre can use a chip kick or a grubber kick to put the ball in the space just behind the defence where it may be regathered and the attack continued behind the main defensive line.

Attack pressure practices

Note: The numbers refer to the corresponding practice games in part II.
Small-sided games:
Handling (1–10), Running and evasion (all), Continuity (all), Kicking (all)
Games for understanding:
38, 39, 41, 42, 43, 48

DEFENCE

TACKLING

Often tackles made by a centre are made on an opponent running at speed. Therefore, the tackle technique of the centre must be excellent, to avoid being sidestepped or brushed aside. The most common tackle made by a centre is the front-on tackle, on an attacker running straight at him. This takes some bravery, but also real concentration on good technique.

Key factors for front tackle:

- Advance towards the attacker, close down the space.

- Just before contact, shorten the stride and sink the hips.

- Keep the head up, chin off chest, eyes on the target, and spine straight.

- Shrug the shoulders, with head to one side of the attackers hips, not across the runner's body. (If tackling with the right shoulder, the head goes to the left of the attacker.)

- Shoulder makes contact above the runner's knees and below his chest (the lower in that target area, the more effective the tackle will usually be).

- Wrap the arms around the runner and squeeze with the arms.

- Use the runner's momentum to bring him down, twisting slightly to land on top of him.

- Release the tackled player, get back on the feet quickly and contest the position from the onside if possible.

Defence pressure practices
Small-sided games:
Tackling (all)
Games for understanding:
37, 44, 46, 47, 50

POSITIONAL VARIATIONS

There are some differences between the tactical demands of inside centre and outside centre, although this can be dependent on the tactical aims of the team's attack.

INSIDE CENTRE (NO. 12)

The inside centre will often choose to attack the space just to the outside of the fly-half. The objective of this run is to 'hold' the opposition defensive line and stop them deliberately drifting the play towards the touchline. Having taken this line, the inside centre must be committed to keeping the ball available by:

- breaking the line (best outcome);

- taking the tackle and offloading to support players in space (next best outcome);

- if these options are not available, to take contact as a maul or ruck, draw defenders to the area, with the aim of creating space and attacking opportunities elsewhere.

To do this, the centre needs to be strong and able to identify space in a congested area, with the agility to move through that space. The aim of the hard-running inside centre is to get ahead of his forward pack and provide a target for the next phase of play: a ruck or a maul.

The inside centre may also be used as a distributor from first and second phase – almost as a second fly-half. In this case, the inside centre lies a little deeper to allow him to identify and pass to runners in space. In so doing, he must have the ability to identify and exploit space:

- between defenders, where the centre attacks the space himself;

- on the outside of the defence, where the centre has the option to pass the ball to put a player into the space;

- behind the defence, where the centre may try to chip or grubber kick to get the ball behind them.

OUTSIDE CENTRE (NO. 13)

The outside centre usually receives the ball a little wider and often in more space than the inside centre. This means that he can be either the clinical finisher, using his elusive running skills to use space created by players inside, or the creator, timing a pass and preserving space for strike runners outside him.

A key area of an outside centre's tactical game is the ability to recognise the shape of the defence in front of him. He must recognise if the defence is drifting across and pushing the attack to the touchline, in which case he should straighten the attack and look to break past the inside shoulders of defenders. Or maybe the defence are stretched and struggling to cover space on the outside, in which case the outside centre should look to check the remaining defenders, committing them to the tackle, before releasing a pass to the winger outside.

CHAPTER 03
FLY-HALF

GENERAL

The fly-half (also known as the 'outside-half' or 'stand-off') is one of the most influential positions on the pitch. A pivotal link between back play and forward play, the fly-half must have great tactical awareness and a well-developed understanding of the game. This means having an awareness of:

- the direction of play (left or right);

- the width of the play (close or wide);

- the use of the forwards for successive attacks;

- moving the ball out to the backs;

- whether to kick for space or for tactical advantage (short or long);

- using his speed, strength and agility as a deceptive runner, to run the ball at the defence in search of weaknesses within the defensive line.

Vision and ability to make quick, accurate decisions, in both attack and defensive play, are core skills of the fly-half. These decisions should be based upon where space exists – in front, to the side or behind defenders – in order to direct the attack into areas of weakness.

In defence, the fly-half is central to applying pressure to the opposition. As an organiser, he is central to controlling the pace and structure of the defence, and, as a tackler, to defending in vulnerable areas of the field close to scrum, line-out, maul and ruck. Strong leadership and self-assurance are good attributes for the fly-half.

Above all, the fly-half needs to control the game and impose a style of play that helps the team dominate the game. Good communication to the players around him is essential to make sure they understand and can execute the tactical decisions being made. In particular, the fly-half must have good communication with the scrum-half so that each knows exactly where the other is at all times.

HANDLING

The fly-half needs to have excellent catching ability to receive a range of passes under pressure. He requires subtlety, dexterity and quick hands to move the ball to the two centres, executing passes of varying weight and length. He must also have the ability to keep the ball available in tight situations when playing very close to defenders. Fundamental to this is the need to have vision – to recognise space and deliver passes both long and short in front of attackers, so that they may penetrate weaknesses in the defensive wall.

RUNNING AND EVASION

A key skill of the fly-half is the ability to accelerate quickly off the mark, to sidestep, change direction and swerve, in order to take advantage of opportunities to attack and find available spaces within a defensive line. The player must also have the determination and courage to support other backs in attack who have initiated a move.

ATTACK

The decision-making ability of the fly-half, together with the ability of support players to react, will affect how close to the gain line the fly-half can play. Generally the closer to the gain line the fly-half chooses to play, the greater the direct threat to the defence. However, playing close to the gain line can have risks. It requires a high level of skill from the fly-half and support players to create attacking opportunities in the reduced space close to the opposition.

Alternatively, the fly-half may choose to play more conservatively, making measured passes to players who will set targets to control the defence and provide options for the following attacking phase. The fly-half may also decide to play further behind the gain line (deep) and use the back line and support players to act as 'option' runners to run a variety of attacking lines. This will help to manipulate the defence and create space for penetrators to attack. Whatever the decision made, the fly-half needs to strike a balance and demonstrate a variety of decisions that keep the opposition guessing.

Attack pressure practices

Note: The numbers refer to the corresponding practice games in part II.
Small-sided games:
Handling (1–10), Running and evasion (all), Continuity (all)
Games for understanding:
38, 39, 41, 42, 43

DEFENCE

The fly-half plays a full role in defence as a tackler and will help to coordinate back-line defence from set pieces through communication with the back-row and centre partnership. There are a range of defensive patterns that might be adopted by the defensive line and these are covered in part II of this book. The fly-half must be familiar with each of these defensive options and when to use the different types of defence. In addition the fly-half is expected to show leadership, courage and strength as generally one of the first-up players in defence.

Defence pressure practices
Small-sided games:
Tackling (all)
Games for understanding:
37, 44, 46, 47, 50

KICKING

The fly-half should be a competent kicker and have the ability to kick out of the hand with either foot and with accuracy and control. He should be able to make high hanging kicks to put the opposition under pressure, while allowing time for attackers to compete for possession. If the defence advances quickly the fly-half may choose to chip or grubber kick and put the ball into space behind the defenders. The aim is to get supporting players past their opponents and regain possession behind the defensive wall with a clear run for the line. Diagonal and line kicks are used to gain territory deep into the opponents' half. The fly-half must be expert at kicking and regularly practise the skills needed to make all forms of kicks. Games should be used to develop the fly-half's ability to kick accurately and under pressure.

Kicking pressure practices
Small-sided games:
Kicking (all)
Games for understanding:
48

CHAPTER 04
SCRUM-HALF

GENERAL
The scrum-half is a key player in the team as a leader, decision- and play-maker, and a link between the forwards and the three-quarters. As link player, the scrum-half must have exceptional passing skills and be able to deliver passes of varying length, with accuracy and to both sides. As leader, the scrum-half is a key communicator, encouraging and directing the efforts of the forwards and three-quarters alike. The scrum-half must have a high degree of vision and alertness to recognise and react quickly to situations in all areas of play. In fact, such is the potential influence of the scrum-half, he should always pose a threat to the opposition, whether he has the ball or not.

In defence, the scrum-half is central to organising the team's cover to ensure gaps are plugged and pressure is applied to the opposition. The scrum-half's personal role in defence is generally as a sweep defender who operates around the fringes of play or behind the main defensive line, offering a second line of defence against line-breaks.

ATTACK

HANDLING/RUNNING AND EVASION

The scrum-half must be able to pass the ball quickly, without delay and to both sides. Reading the situation quickly, he must be able to execute an appropriate pass – standing, spin, pivot, dive and reverse – to supporting players to gain maximum advantage from the situation. The speed and accuracy of the pass is more important than its length, although a longer pass can be an advantage, as the ball is received further from the potential threat posed by opposition forwards. The scrum-half should also have the evasive skills, pace, power and acceleration to exploit gaps in the opponents' defence, especially around the fringes of a scrum, maul or ruck. The scrum-half should practise the skills needed to develop his ability to beat an opponent 'one on one', even in the most restricted areas.

KICKING

Ideally, the scrum-half should be able to kick with either foot and be able to execute a range of kicks based on the situation: clearing, box, chip and grubber. In many situations, the scrum-half operates behind the breakdown, scrum or line-out and should be practiced at kicking from these situations to gain advantage or to relieve pressure. There should also be an appreciation of the differing conditions within a game, such as wet or windy, and how these might impact on the type of kick used.

Attack pressure practices

Note: The numbers refer to the corresponding practice games in part II.
Small-sided games:
Handling (1–10), Running and evasion (all), Continuity (all), Kicking (all), Scrum (31)
Games for understanding:
38, 39, 41, 42, 43, 48

DEFENCE

In scrum defence, the scrum-half will generally attempt to apply pressure to the opponents by following the ball to the back of the opposing scrum and trying to reduce space and time for the opposing scrum-half or back row to move the ball away or to create an attack from the scrum. In either case, the scrum-half must work with his own back row to form a strong defensive unit. For example:

- If the opposition decides to launch an attack direct from the scrum, the scrum-half, working with the back row, is often the first line of defence and must be an effective tackler; this will frequently be against forwards much bigger than himself.

- If the opposition chooses to pass the ball away from the scrum, the scrum-half and back row provide a cover defence, guarding against line-breaks and remaining close to the ball to launch counter-attacks if a tackle results in a turnover in possession.

It follows that the scrum-half must be a tenacious and effective tackler and should also practise scrum defence with the back row so that the role of each player in different situations becomes instinctive.

In rucks and mauls, the scrum-half is likely to be the defensive organiser. He should understand and communicate the defensive options in order to apply pressure to the opposition; where necessary, he should provide the cover defence should the opposition break the first line of defence. At all times, the team should be looking at turning defence into attack, with the scrum-half being instrumental in the decision-making and distribution of the ball away from contact.

Defence pressure practices

Small-sided games:
Tackling (all)
Games for understanding:
37, 44, 46, 47, 50

CHAPTER 05
PROP FORWARD

GENERAL

Prop forwards are the strongmen of any rugby team: big, durable and powerful individuals. However, these qualities must not be the only considerations. The modern prop also has to be mobile and athletic, with well-developed ball-handling skills to be able to contribute and be effective in all areas of the game.

Due to the nature and physical demands of front-row play and the confrontational demands of scrummaging, props need to have certain mental characteristics that set them apart from their teammates. They must enjoy the physical contest of both strength and technique and be resilient and mentally tough enough to deal with intense moments of concentration and pressure in all set pieces, especially the scrum.

The modern prop forward will also be expected to contribute to the team outside of the set piece. The ability to carry the ball in open play and manage it in contact are core skills of the prop, as is the ability to deliver and receive passes under pressure. Props will also be involved in a high percentage of rucks and mauls and they need to transfer the skills that they use at the scrum into these areas of the contact game. The prop should also be a strong defender and is expected to make many tackles during the game.

General pressure practices
Note: The numbers refer to the corresponding practice games in part II.
Small-sided games:
Handling (all), Running and evasion (all), Continuity (all), Tackling (all)
Games for understanding:
37, 41, 42, 45, 50

SCRUM
Each scrum has two props: the loose head packs down on the left-hand side of the scrum (No. 1), with the tight head on the right (No. 3).

While the two positions have slight differences with regard to binding and positioning, both props generally have similar skills and attributes and should be equally comfortable playing on either side of the scrum. Props form the foundation of the scrum and their main role is to channel the weight and power of the other players, in a coordinated drive, through to the opposition. In an attacking scrum they also provide a stable platform for the hooker to strike and win the ball.

SCRUM TECHNIQUE PRACTICES

Scrum practices should always be supervised by a qualified coach.

Scrummaging should be practised individually and collectively; the coach should help the props develop their ability to manage their own body weight so that they can maintain the basic body shape shown in the picture below. When this basic technique has been mastered, the coach will encourage the prop to test those skills one on one against an opponent. As the props become more confident, they can then practise as a front row unit or as a scrummaging unit with their second row and flanker. Eventually, they can practise as a full pack, with the coach getting the players familiar with, and using, the engagement process of 'CROUCH, TOUCH, PAUSE, ENGAGE'.

Scrum pressure practices
Small-sided games:
Scrum (all)

LINE-OUT

Props have a vital role to play at line-out, where they will generally take on a main support role to secure or create a stable platform once the ball has been caught. Above the Under-16 age group, when lifting in the line-out is permitted, it is often the props who take on the lion's share of the lifting duties, lifting and supporting jumpers as they challenge for the ball in the air. To do this, they must practise and coordinate their ability to move and lift with the other members of the line-out. They must develop their strength and technique to execute a safe and effective lift and be quick across the ground to react to the evasive movement of the jumper. Lifting in the line-out is a skill that needs to be practised on a regular basis; props need to become familiar with the speed of movement and the technique of the jumper, and react to both the foot movement and verbal instructions of the jumper.

RESTARTS

These same skills are often employed when the team is receiving kick-offs. Receivers will often position themselves under the kick-off or drop-out and jump to win the ball to beat the oncoming chasers. As in the line-out, props must react to the receiver's movements and also read the flight of the ball in order to lift the jumper and help him to claim the ball for their team.

OPEN PLAY

While the core skills needed for the line-out and scrum are important, props have to be fully integrated into all other elements of play. They must be effective ball carriers and tacklers, where they can use their strength and power as dynamic weapons in both attack and defence. The props' strength and front-row skills will also be put to good use in breakdowns and contact areas: they often find themselves at the front of driven mauls, especially from the line-out, and at the ruck area, where they can move opponents quickly and efficiently using the strength in their shoulders, legs, back, neck and arms.

Line-out pressure practices
Small-sided games:
Line-out (33, 34, 35)
Games for understanding:
40

CHAPTER 06
HOOKER

GENERAL
The hooker has one of the most demanding positions in the game. Often used as a fourth back-row player, the hooker must have the endurance of a flanker, combined with the strength and dynamism of a prop, in order to add to the effectiveness of the front row of the scrum.

Aggressive, dynamic and fully committed in contact, the hooker also has to demonstrate some of the most technically difficult skills in the game. At the line-out, often under extreme pressure, the hooker must deliver an accurate throw for the jumpers to secure clean and dependable possession. At scrum, under the static pressure of the front row, the hooker must be able to coordinate his strike to the scrum-half's feed and accurately direct the ball to the back row of the scrum. Of all the players, the hooker must be able to shift both mentally and emotionally from the often highly charged situations at ruck, maul and tackle to the relative calmness and discipline needed to throw at the line-out. Establishing routines at the line-out and scrum often helps hookers to improve their control in these two critical areas of the game. These should be practised regularly in training, and most hookers prefer to go through line-out and scrum routines as part of their warm-up activities before a game.

In general play, much of the hooker's game mirrors the back row and, for general training patterns, he should carry out the same exercises and practices as described in the back-row chapter.

General pressure practices

Note: The numbers refer to the corresponding practice games in part II.
Small-sided games:
Handling (all), Running and evasion (all), Continuity (all), Tackling (all)
Games for understanding:
37, 41, 42, 45, 50

SCRUM

The scrum is one of the areas of play that defines rugby union and all hookers are encouraged to pay great attention to perfecting their technique in this area. Every scrum is important and establishing a set routine for the play is a good way of reminding players of the discipline and concentration needed to be effective. Scrummaging should be practised regularly to remind players of their roles and also to reinforce the safety aspects relating to the scrum. Even in training, it should be 'refereed' properly to avoid serious injury and practised under game levels of fatigue to ensure that players perform with the same attention to detail.

SCRUM SETUP

Building the scrum starts with the hooker and, because of this central role, he often leads and captains the scrum formation. In this role, and working with the referee, the hooker will communicate and coordinate the formation of his side's scrum to make sure that the scrum engagement is carried out safely and as a unit. This requires all players in the scrum to adopt a good scrum body position; in training, this safe body position should be regularly practised and repeated until it becomes second nature for all scrum players.

In the scrum, the hooker strikes for the ball (usually with his right foot) and propels it through the loose-head prop's legs to the back of the scrum. The pace and direction of the ball as it goes through the scrum is key to the scrum's effectiveness, and the hooker should practise with the scrum-half to perfect hooking of the ball.

Initially, this can be practised with the hooker (leaning against a post or upright) and scrum-half working together to perfect the timing of the 'strike', before building this practice up to full scrum conditions.

Scrum pressure practices
Small-sided games:
Scrum (all)

LINE-OUT

The hooker generally throws in at the line-out. This is a precise and very important skill as the quality of the throw has a direct bearing on the ability of the line-out jumpers to win the ball. Indeed, given the number of line-outs in a game and the attacking opportunities that they offer, there are those who argue that the ability to throw is the single most important skill of a hooker.

With practice, the hooker should be able to deliver the ball to each of the jumpers in the line-out in a way that is tailored to that jumper. This may involve practising throws of different heights and speeds, and often with a degree of disguise. Simple practices and warm-ups can involve throwing to fixed points, such as the posts or throwing targets, to refine the throwing technique. But even in practice, it is important to progress to repeated drills for all variations of the throw and under physical and mental conditions, for example fatigue and muscle tiredness, similar to those of a match.

Throwing requires not only skill but also resilience and mental toughness to not let a bad throw affect the player's game and confidence. With regular practice and adherence to a routine, it is likely that they will be able to increase their success rate at throwing. Like goal kickers, it is suggested that some golden rules are followed to develop a good basic technique. Here is an example of a checklist to develop good throwing technique:

- Ball is held stable before and during the throw, most commonly with two hands on the ball.

- Ball is gripped securely by spreading the fingers and thumbs.

- Feet are shoulder width apart and as level as possible to avoid undue rotation of the hips.

- Feet, hips, chest, shoulders and head should all face the intended target of the throw.

- Ball should be held above the head and with the elbows as close together as is comfortable (see figure above).

- Throw is initiated by bending the knees, then pulling on the abdominal muscles, also known as the front 'core' muscles, as the arms arc in a straight line over the head to ensure the throw is delivered in a straight line.

- Drive should then go up through the body finishing with the wrist and fingers.

- Finish position for the throw is on the balls of the feet.

Practise throwing while sitting or kneeling on a Swiss ball: this is a great way to strengthen the throwing muscles and improve core strength.

Line-out pressure practices
Small-sided games:
Line-out (36)
Games for understanding:
40

CHAPTER 07
SECOND ROW

GENERAL

The two second-row players, the locks, are sometimes referred to as the engine room of the team. Often the biggest players on the pitch in terms of height, weight and strength, they also need to be athletic and skilful, have good handling and running skills, and be sound defenders. The position of the second row is surely one of the most demanding in the game as they also need mental flexibility to move straight from tackling, mauling and scrum work, to using evasive movement and deft handling skills needed to win the line-out.

General pressure practices
Note: The numbers refer to the corresponding practice games in part II.
Small-sided games:
Handling (all), Running and evasion (all), Continuity (all), Tackling (all)
Games for understanding:
37, 41, 42, 45, 50

SCRUM
The lock must have excellent scrum skills to be able to work with the front row to provide forward power in the scrum. To a large extent it is the second-row players who provide the stability to the scrum, working together as a pair to keep the drive straight and in a forward direction. It is the ability to keep the scrum stable that maximises the drive and force generated at the second row. To achieve this and maintain an effective drive, the locks should practise on both the right- and left-hand sides of the scrum and be able to adapt to different scrum conditions and the opposition.

SCRUM SETUP
Practising the formation of the scrum is crucial. The second row binds to the front row before the scrum engagement and plays a key role in making sure the props and hooker are balanced prior to the engagement. This means that the second row must be able to stabilise the prop's weight as well as controlling their own body position in readiness for the engagement. This must be practised regularly and repeated until it becomes routine, as a good, stable platform prior to engagement is a key factor in safe and effective scrummaging.

BODY POSITION AND DRIVE
Maintaining a good body position as shown in the figure below is crucial not only to provide maximum drive but also for personal safety. This body position helps to protect the neck, shoulders and spine during scrummaging and should be practised under the guidance of an experienced coach until perfected.

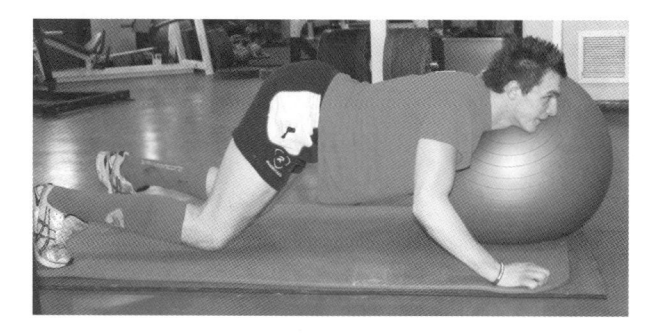

Once the correct body position is perfected, there are a number of exercises that can be performed individually or in small groups to develop a player's ability to maintain body shape during the action of driving. The aim of these exercises is not only to develop a good body position but also to work on maintaining it during the dynamic action of driving. This picture shows the scrum position for the power crawl and tyre push.

Scrum pressure practices
Small-sided games:
Scrum (all)

LINE-OUT

Up to the Under-16 age group, lifting in the line-out is not permitted and, in these younger age groups, it is generally the tallest in the team, the locks and number 8, who are the targets for the throw into the line-out. Above the Under-16 age group, the inclusion of supported jumpers gives more variation to the line-out and players generally have a dual role, as both jumper and support player.

At all ages, the jumpers in the line-out should be encouraged to move and evade opposing jumpers so that they jump and take the ball in areas of the line-out where there are no competing catchers. To do this, the lock needs to be dynamic in his footwork to enable him to move and jump with explosive speed and power. Training with ladders or cones helps to encourage short dynamic steps and quick movement and improve the ability of the lock to get off the ground quickly. These techniques should be perfected by the individual and built up to include the movement of support and option players in the full line-out.

RESTARTS

Due to their physical presence, the locks are key players at the restart, both in attacking the kick-off and in kick-off receipt. The skills needed at the restart are generally the same as for the line-out and the lock should practise catching a high ball as often as possible. This is an individual skill, but at kick-off the lock may also work with a support player and so practices should include movement and communication in order to be effective as a catching or challenging team.

OPEN PLAY

In open-field play, the lock should develop himself as a mixture of a front-row and back-row player. He should develop the same combative and abrasive skills as the prop, while also sharing the defensive and attacking qualities and athleticism of the back-row player. The lock should, therefore, join in and compete in practices with the prop forward and back row.

Line-out pressure practices

Small-sided games:
Line-out (33, 34, 35)
Games for understanding:
40

CHAPTER 08
BACK ROW

GENERAL
The three back-row forwards are some of the most versatile of all rugby players. Spending much of their time working in the forward pack, they must also have pace, handling and evasion skills to fit seamlessly into back-line moves. As the 'back row' in the scrum, and often at the tail of the line-out, the back row has the clearest view and most direct route to support and defend play from both scrum and line-out. This predatory role is now extended to all facets of the game and it is expected that the back row will be close in support of all plays.

It is this extreme work rate and athleticism that makes a good back-row player. Often tall to provide options as a line-out jumper, the back-row player has muscular strength for contact, pace to be first in support, and endurance to last the whole 80 minutes. The back row must have the ability to pass and receive the ball with both hands over short and long distances, and as a key player in the contact area he must be expert in the offload pass before and after contact.

TACKLING

This is perhaps the most important part of back-row play. In defence it is the aim of a back-row player to stay close enough to the ball carrier to be the principal threat as tackler and ball winner. The back-row player must be quick to get into position to make an effective tackle and be physically strong to drive through the tackle and bring the ball carrier to the ground. Having completed the tackle, the back row should be single-minded in its effort to contest for the ball.

CONTACT SKILLS: RUCKING AND MAULING

Generally one of the first players to arrive at any situation, the back-row player needs to be able to read the situation quickly and decide on the most effective course of action. Based on what the player sees and the proximity of defenders, availability of the ball, state of the game and conditions, he has to make a quick decision on what to do to get the best outcome from the situation.

These decision-making processes and the contact skills are critical for the back-row player to be effective. The player needs to recognise when it is right to offload before contact or to make contact and drive; whether to ruck or to maul; to clear players away from the contact area or, if there is space, to pick up and drive. These are complex decisions made in the last few metres as the player approaches the contact area and should be practised and simulated regularly in training until they become instinctive.

General pressure practices

Note: The numbers refer to the corresponding practice games in part II.
Small-sided games:
Handling (all), Running and evasion (all), Continuity (all), Tackling (all)
Games for understanding:
37, 41, 42, 45, 50

SCRUM

The back row must understand the basic mechanics and good body positions needed for effective scrummaging. This is so they can use their power and drive to keep the scrum stable and provide forward pressure. Positioned behind the outside buttock of each prop, the flankers drive inwards at a slight angle to counter the push of the second row on the props, as shown below. The flanker binds with his arm across the back of the nearest second-row player and will take up a dynamic, low driving position. This not only gives stability to the scrum but is also an active starting position for the flanker to break from it and be first to the next phase of play as soon as the ball is clear.

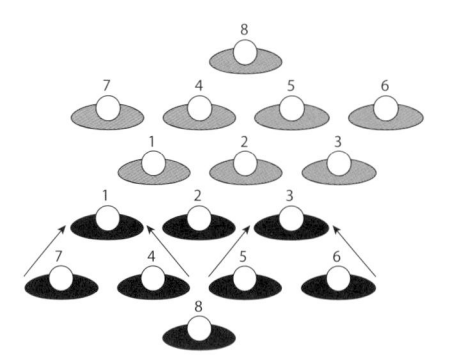

The number 8 provides the control and is often the key decision-maker in choosing how to attack from the scrummage. Working closely with the scrum-half, he will decide how to maximise attacking opportunities from the scrum.

Generally the number 8 binds between the two second-row players. However, in 'open age' rugby the laws allow the number 8 to bind between the left-hand second-row player and flanker; this is to take advantage of a quicker ball won in the scrum. The overall contribution of the back row to the power should not be underestimated and can be the difference between gaining scrum advantage and being under pressure in both attack and defence.

In attack and with the ball secured there are generally two options. The first is to move the ball quickly to the backs, in which case the flankers and number 8 will run in support and follow the ball, aiming to be first to support and provide continuity in play. The second option is for the number 8 to pick the ball up and run a play from the base of the scrum: here the aim, with the support of the flankers, is to gain territory close to the scrum, commit defenders and release the ball to support players to exploit the space created by this 'back-row' move.

In defence at the scrum, it is the back row that sets the foundation of the team's defence. Before leaving the scrum, these players must first guard against a direct attack from an opposing back-row move. Working as a team they must move quickly to cut down space and defend the side of the scrum under attack.

If the attacking team chooses to pass the ball away from the scrum, it is the back-row players' job to provide support to their own back line to defend against midfield attacks. In this situation it is the role of the open-side flanker (No. 7) to follow the ball, while the number 8 and the blind-side flanker (No. 6) take complementary running lines to guard against potential line-breaks or players cutting back against the flow of play. All three back-row players provide tackling support and should be first to the breakdown to make the most of any advantage.

Scrum pressure practices
Small-sided games:
Scrum (all)

LINE-OUT

The back-row players are broadly interchangeable at the line-out. They should all be coached in the skills and techniques needed to jump and catch, block and support players, and provide different options for ball winning. With this in mind, they should join in coaching practices with the other line-out players to perfect the options at the line-out. This role is well suited to the back-row players as they are athletic and aggressive as jumpers, and strong and uncompromising as support players and blockers.

Back-row players are generally the fastest forwards on the field and for this reason there is usually one of them at the tail of the line-out. In attack from the line-out, it is the role of the back row, once the ball has left the line-out, to work hard to get close to the ball carrier or to be first to the breakdown.

The laws of the line-out insist on a minimum of 20 metres between opposing backs. In defence, this has a major impact as it is the player at the tail of the line-out who is likely to be the closest player to the attackers and can pose the greatest defensive threat. In this picture, we can see No. 7 tracking the ball and working with his No. 8 to reduce space for the attackers to work in.

Line-out pressure practices
Small-sided games:
Line-out (33, 34, 35)
Games for understanding:
40

POSITIONAL VARIATIONS

BLIND-SIDE FLANKER (NO. 6)

The blind-side flanker is the real workhorse in the back row. As the name suggests, he packs down on the blind side of the scrum and is the first defender against attacking moves in this area. Often physically the bigger of the two flankers, the blind-side flanker frequently finds himself just behind the first wave of support, with vision and time to make a real impact on play. He must have the ability to read the game well and have exceptional skills to recognise and react to close-quarter variations in play. At line-out the blind-side flanker usually has the physical attributes to be used as a jumper or support player and should be well practised in both these roles.

OPEN-SIDE FLANKER (NO. 7)

The open-side flanker is often the quickest player in the back row. At scrum he packs on the side closest to the three-quarters' lines and at line-out he is generally at the 'tail' of the line-out. In general, it is the open-side flanker's job to anticipate and use his speed to get into a supporting position near the ball carrier. In defence, he can be the most destructive of defenders, shadowing the ball at pace and looking to tackle any opponent he can catch in possession. Fearless in contact and single-minded in pursuit of the ball, the open-side flanker lives on the edge. He must understand and use the laws of the game to his advantage to contest for the ball or compete to be first to the next phase of play.

NUMBER 8 (NO. 8)

The number 8 is the player who provides balance and organisation at the back of the scrum. Usually tall and athletic, he plays a central role in dictating play from scrum and is also often used as a main target jumper in the line-out. The number 8 must be tactically very aware and a good reader of the game, as his decisions often dictate and set the direction of play, particularly from scrum.

PART TWO
PRACTICES

CHAPTER 09
SMALL-SIDED GAMES

Coaching best practice promotes greater use of conditioned and small-sided games to improve a player's techniques and skills. The added benefit of coaching through games is that, at the same time, players develop tactical awareness and tend to be more motivated by the competitive and fun elements of the activity.

In this book 'small-sided games' refers to games for up to six players. Many of these games can be tailored to serve as warm-up activities, or adapted into general fun games that can be played in the garden or park with friends to further encourage players to develop their own skills.

However, where games have safety or contact implications, such as scrums or tackles, these must be monitored and supervised by a qualified and experienced coach. In this book, for activities where this applies, the exercises are clearly marked and must be supervised by an appropriately qualified coach.

HANDLING

Practice games in this section:

1. Piggy in the middle
2. Touch ground-pass
3. Handling under pressure
4. Receive and pass
5. 2 v 1
6. 3 v 2
7. Standing scrum-half pass without back lift
8. Pass and move using scrum-half pass
9. General handling skills
10. Restarts: Catching a high ball
11. Restarts: Jumping to catch, supported

SMALL-SIDED GAMES

PRACTICE 1

Title: Piggy in the middle (Can also be used as a good warm-up game)	Time: 10 minutes
	Kit: Balls, bibs, cones
Objective: Improve basic core handling skills	Organisation: Groups of 4–6
Game Principles: Pressure, support and continuity	Grid Size: 10m x 10m
Description: <ul><li>Stop the defender from getting the ball</li><li>Pass between the attackers</li><li>Once the defender intercepts the ball, the passer or last player in contact with the ball is in the middle</li></ul>	
Relevant Positions: Back three, centre, fly-half, scrum-half, prop forward, hooker, second row, back row	

Increase Difficulty:	• Reduce the grid size • Introduce an extra ball	Decrease Difficulty:	• Increase the grid size • Condition movement of defenders

Key Coaching Points / Questions:

- Hands up ready to receive, 'W' shape (palms facing towards the ball, thumbs touching, fingers pointing up) in front of the chest
- Move on balls of feet in readiness to react
- Develop vision to be able to keep an eye on the ball and the players who are free to receive a pass – chin off chest
- Shape the body for the pass to ensure ball transfers across the body
- Accuracy of pass to recipient's hands
- Elbows close to the body
- Soft hands and use of fingers for short passes
- Follow through with the pass

PRACTICE 2

Title: Touch ground-pass *(Can also be used as a good warm-up game)*	Time: 10 minutes
	Kit: Balls, bibs, cones
Objective: Improve basic core handling skills	Organisation: Groups of 4–6
Game Principles: Pressure, support and continuity	Grid Size: 10m x 10m
Description: <ul><li>One team touches the ground and passes ball to own team, each complete pass is 1 point</li><li>Once 5 points are reached, the ball swaps to the opposition</li><li>Opposing teams try to stop the completion of passes</li><li>If ball is intercepted, the intercepting team takes over possession and therefore scoring</li></ul>		
Relevant Positions: Back three, centre, fly-half, scrum-half, prop forward, hooker, second row, back row		

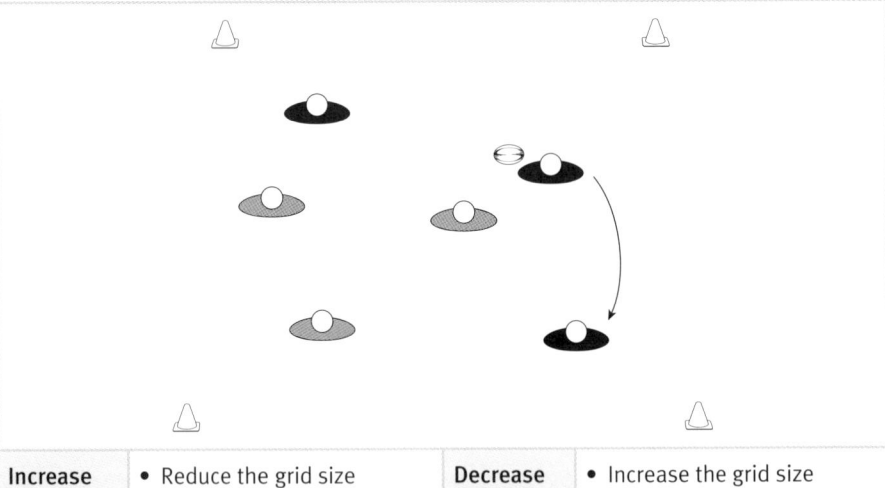

Increase Difficulty:	• Reduce the grid size • Introduce an extra ball	Decrease Difficulty:	• Increase the grid size • Condition movement of defenders

Key Coaching Points / Questions:

- Hands up ready to receive, 'W' shape in front of the chest
- Move on balls of feet in readiness to react
- Develop vision to be able to keep an eye on the ball and the players who are free to receive a pass – chin off chest
- Shape the body for the pass to ensure ball transfers across the body
- Accuracy of pass to recipient's hands
- Elbows close to the body
- Soft hands (relaxed) and use of fingers for short passes (not palms)
- Follow through with the pass

SMALL-SIDED GAMES

Progression 1:
Reduce grid size to work on evasion skills close to defenders.

Progression 2:
Increase grid size to work on length and accuracy of pass.

PRACTICE 3

Title: Handling under pressure	**Time:** 5 minutes
	Kit: 2 balls
Objective: Develop vision and handling ability under pressure	**Organisation:** Groups of 4
Game Principles: Support and continuity	**Grid Size:** 10m x 15m in diameter

Description:
- Three players (two with a ball) stand in a semi-circle approximately 5m in radius
- Target player stands in the middle
- Pass is played to the target player who passes the ball immediately back to the only player without a ball who is not the player who has just passed the ball
- As soon as the pass has been made, the next ball is passed to the target player and the game continues

Relevant Positions: Back three, centre, fly-half, scrum-half, prop forward, hooker, second row, back row

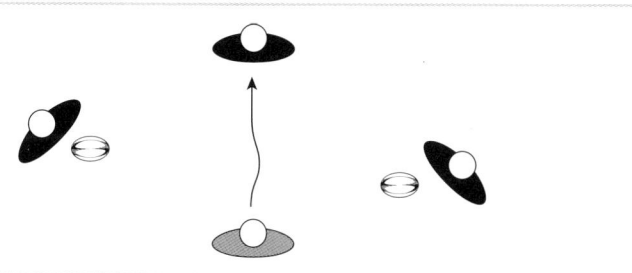

49

Increase Difficulty:	• Increase the size of the circle • Increase the number of balls in the circle • Player in the middle to perform other skills	Decrease Difficulty:	• Reduce the size of the circle • Begin with just one ball

Key Coaching Points / Questions:

- Hands up ready to receive, 'W' shape in front of the chest.
- All players on balls of feet in readiness to react
- Develop vision to be able to keep an eye on the ball and the players who are free to receive a pass – chin off chest
- Accuracy of pass to recipient's hands
- Elbows close to the body
- Soft hands (relaxed) and use of fingers for short passes (not palms)
- Follow through with the pass

Progression 1:
Vary the feed so that the player in the middle has to react to a high or low pass or to one that has bounced.

Progression 2:
Increase the size of the circle so that longer passes can be made. Allow middle player in receipt of the ball two steps to assist in the delivery of the pass. He must always return to the middle to receive a further pass.

Progression 3:
After completing a pass, the player must touch the floor prior to receiving the next pass. Player will need to work on getting into a good receiving position quickly.

PRACTICE 4

Title: Receive and pass

Time: 5–10 minutes

Kit: 1 ball, cones, coloured markers or pieces of card

Objective: Develop the ability of the player to receive and pass the ball

Organisation: Groups of 4

Game Principles: Go forwards and support

Grid Size: 10m x 10m

Description:
- Player stands at the end of the grid with two players at irregular intervals to the side of the grid
- Nearest of the support players acts as the feeder and passes to the player as he enters the grid
- As the first player moves forwards, he passes the ball to the second player and runs through to the end of the grid
- Player returns to the original position and repeats the drill

Relevant Positions: Back three, centre, fly-half, scrum-half, prop forward, hooker, second row, back row

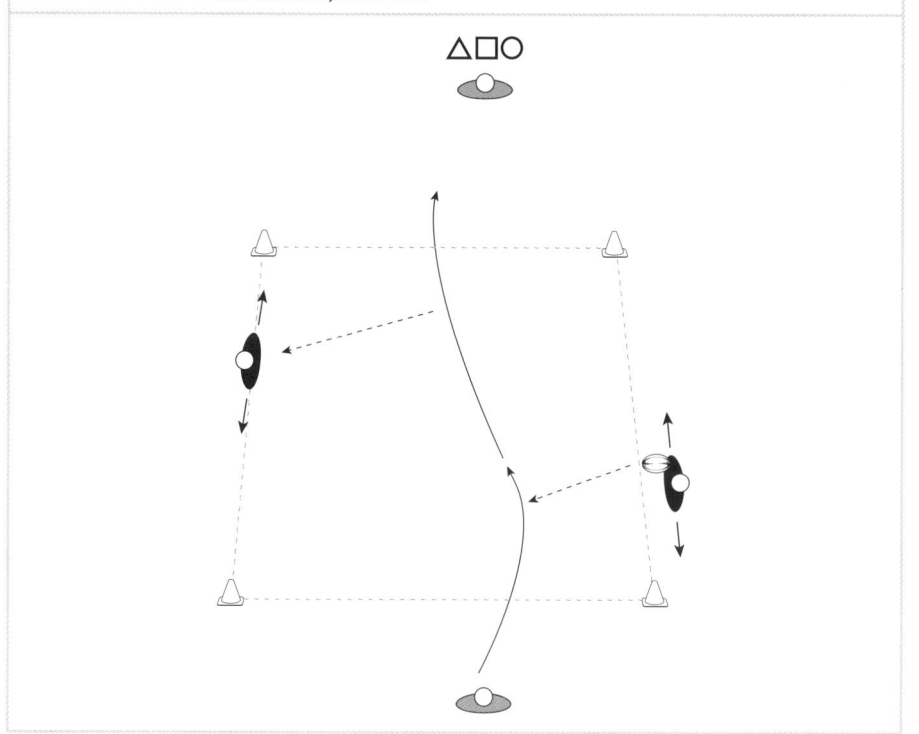

Increase Difficulty:	• Vary feed • Reduce number of steps with the ball • Type of pass	Decrease Difficulty:	• Reduce the size of the grid • Begin with just one ball

Key Coaching Points / Questions:

- Hands up and across the body towards the ball
- Emphasise the outside hand across the body – this will help turn hips towards the ball and open up the body for receipt of the pass
- 'W' shape with the hands
- Elbows tight to the body
- Transfer hands across the body in a straight line
- Rotate the hips towards the receiver as the pass is made

Progression 1:

Add time factor to the exercise: the player has to complete five passes within 30 seconds. Vary the time to develop hands in the pass while maintaining accuracy of pass.

Progression 2:

Vary width of receipt and pass.

Progression 3:

Develop range of passes: flat, deep, 'spin' and 'static'.

Progression 4:

Vary running line on to the ball and after receipt of pass.

Progression 5:

Introduce awareness skills with coach/assistant standing at the end of the grid and holding up coloured cards or shapes. Player to call out colour or shape of card without hesitation or affecting execution of the practice.

PRACTICE 5

Title: 2 v 1	Time: 15 minutes
	Kit: Balls, cones
Objective: Work in a smaller area and improve ability of players to score in a 2 v 1 situation	Organisation: Groups of 3
Game Principles: Go forwards, retain possession and apply pressure	Grid Size: 10m x 10m
Description: • Two attackers and one defender start at the same point, attackers with the ball • The start point can be offset closer to cone 'A' to favour the attackers, or closer to cone 'D' to favour the defenders • Attackers run round cone 'A' and realign to attack try line 'C-D' • Defender runs round cone 'D' and turns to defend try line 'C-D' • Attackers attempt to beat the defender and score • The game is over when either a try is scored or the ball breaks down • Players return to the start point and the exercise is repeated	
Relevant Positions: Back three, centre, fly-half, scrum-half, prop forward, hooker, second row, back row	

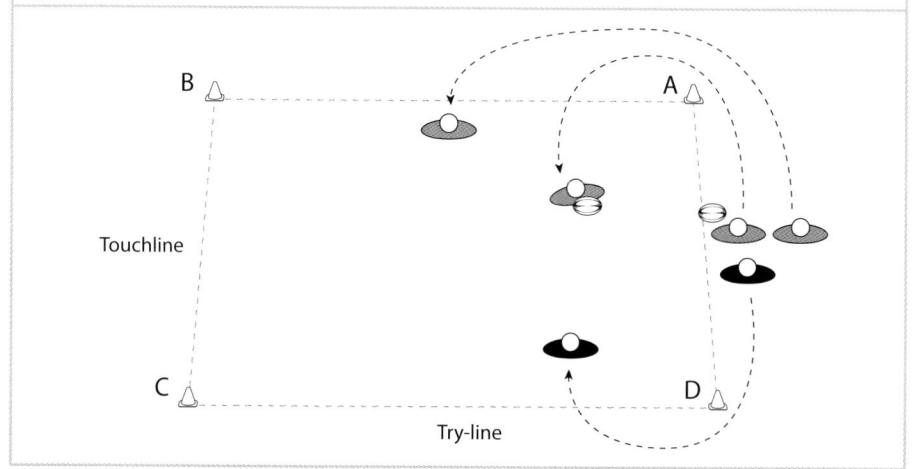

Increase Difficulty:	• Reduce the width of the grid	Decrease Difficulty:	• Make the grid wider • Condition defender to defend in predetermined channels or against certain attackers

Key Coaching Points / Questions:

Attackers

- Communicate attacking options and intentions
- Supporting players maintain depth and communicate position
- Ball carrier moves and 'fixes' the defender to create/preserve space in which to attack
- Ball in two hands and timing of pass so defender does not have time to drift and defend second attacker
- Supporting player moves at pace from deep, with hands up to receive the pass

Defender

- Moves into position quickly
- Tries to 'push' attackers to minimise space for the attack
- Uses touchline 'B-C' as second defender
- Assumes good athletic position ready to tackle
- Demonstrates good tackle technique (see section on tackling)

Progression 1:

Start with 1 v 1 to isolate and correct evasive/attacking lines of running with attackers. Also work with defender on tackle technique and use of touchline as second defender.

Progression 2:

Use a wide grid (15m) to give attackers advantage of space in which to attack. Condition defender to defend certain channels or against predetermined attackers to see reaction of attacking players.

Progression 3:

Narrow the grid to give advantage to the defender and remove any conditions.

SMALL-SIDED GAMES

PRACTICE 6

Title: 3 v 2	Time: 15 minutes
	Kit: Balls, cones
Objective: Work in a smaller area and improve ability to create overlap in a 3 v 2 situation	Organisation: Groups of 5
Game Principles: Go forwards and retain possession	Grid Size: 20m x 20m

Description:
- Attacking players line up on one side of the grid with two defenders on the opposite side of the grid as shown in the figure
- Player at 'F' feeds the ball to any of the three attacking players
- Ball carrier has to choose the right running line to 'fix' the defenders and preserve space to give options to the attack
- Ball carrier must communicate intentions
- Supporting players realign to create an overlap situation and score a try over the defending line of cones
- Players change round and the exercise is repeated

Relevant Positions: Back three, centre, fly-half, scrum-half, prop forward, hooker, second row, back row

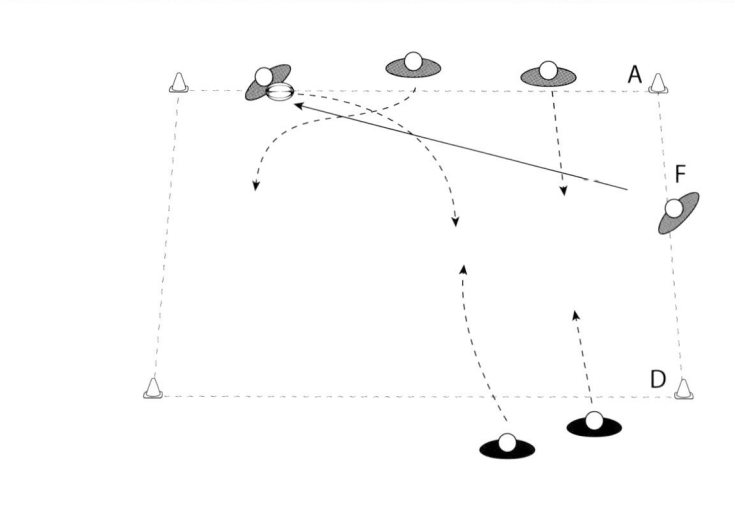

55

Increase Difficulty:	• Reduce the size of the grid • Shorten the distance between attack and defence • Players enter the grid by running from 'F' around corner cone, attackers around 'A' and defenders around 'D'	Decrease Difficulty:	• Make the grid wider • Condition defenders to defend in predetermined channels or against certain attackers

Key Coaching Points / Questions:

- Back three
- Attackers give good clear and decisive call for the ball
- Communicate intentions to the others in the back three
- Ball carrier runs to fix chasing players and preserve space for the attack
- Others realign to provide attacking options and make use of available space for the attack
- Provide continuous support throughout the play

Progression 1:

Coach may start by sending defenders out individually to allow space for the back three to work on counter-attack options.

Progression 2:

Condition defenders to defend certain channels or against predetermined attackers to see reaction of attacking players.

Progression 3:

Narrow the grid to put more pressure on the attackers.

SMALL-SIDED GAMES

PRACTICE 7

Title: Standing scrum-half pass without back lift	Time: 5 minutes
	Kit: 1 ball per group, cones
Objective: Develop standing pass without back lift	Organisation: Groups of 3–5
Game Principles: Possession, go forwards, apply pressure	Grid Size: Triangle with 10m sides or 10m x 10m square

Description:
- Players stand on the corners of the grid
- Scrum-half passes to the first player (player 1) on the grid, who catches the ball and puts it on the ground
- Scrum-half chases the ball, 'sets' and passes to the next player on the grid and the exercise continues
- Once the exercise has been practised, another player can be introduced, who sets off after the scrum-half, applying pressure and reducing the time for the scrum-half to complete the pass
- Delay the run of the chasing player to provide appropriate levels of pressure on the scrum-half

Relevant Positions: Back three, centre, fly-half, scrum-half, prop forward, hooker, second row, back row

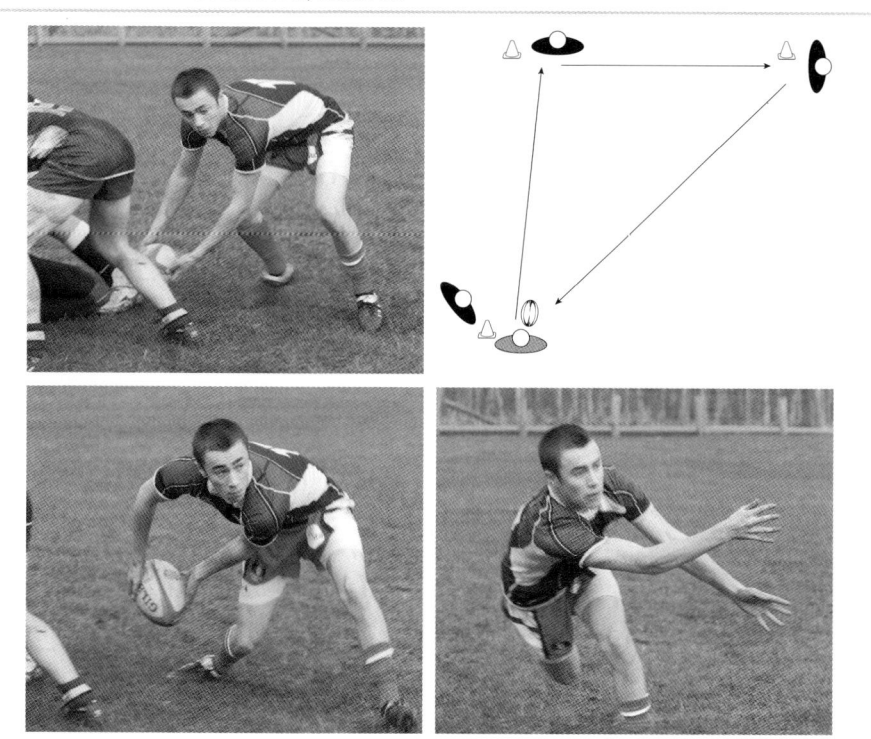

57

| Increase Difficulty: | • Increase the distance between players | Decrease Difficulty: | • Reduce the distance between players |

Key Coaching Points / Questions:

- In the following practices, the rear foot can be considered to be the one closest to the ball and the front foot to be the one that is pointing towards the receiver
- Ball to be placed inside of rear foot
- Feet to be placed apart to provide wide stable base
- Front foot to point towards intended direction of pass and in line with heel of rear foot
- Fingers spread and placed behind the belly of the ball
- Knees flexed to lower the body's centre of gravity
- Hand to push through the ball
- Weight to be transferred across the body during the pass, from rear foot to front foot
- Passing hand to follow through the pass and point at receiver

Progression 1:

Develop standing scrum-half pass using two hands.

Key Coaching Points / Questions:

- Bring second hand onto the ball, hands placed off centre; outside hand towards the rear of the ball and inside hand towards the front
- Pass and transfer of weight to occur at the same time
- Finish with weight on the front foot

Progression 2:

Develop diving pass.

Key Coaching Points / Questions:

- Scrum-half to have feet slight distance apart
- Ball placed lengthways in front of feet
- Knees flexed to lower the centre of gravity
- Hands to be placed either side of the ball
- Scrum-half to drive off feet and move body weight forwards while extending hands towards the target
- Chin off chest and eyes looking at the target
- Hands to follow through and point at receiver

| Increase Difficulty: | • Increase the distance between players
• Drop the ball in front of the player so that he has to react to the bounce of the ball and complete the pass
• This progression requires the player to be on the balls of the feet and to use the feet more to get into the correct position |

PRACTICE 8

Title: Pass and move using scrum-half pass	Time: 5 minutes
(Can also be used as a good warm-up game)	Kit: Ball, bibs, cones
Objective: Develop scrum-half pass within a game	Organisation: Groups of 3–5
Game Principles: Go forwards and support	Grid Size: 30m x 20m

Description:
- Attackers start from their try line and move the ball towards the opposition's try line to score
- Upon receipt of the ball, player to place it on the ground before passing to support
- All passes from the ground – no movement with the ball
- Ball can be passed forwards or backwards

Relevant Positions: Back three, centre, fly-half, scrum-half, prop forward, hooker, second row, back row

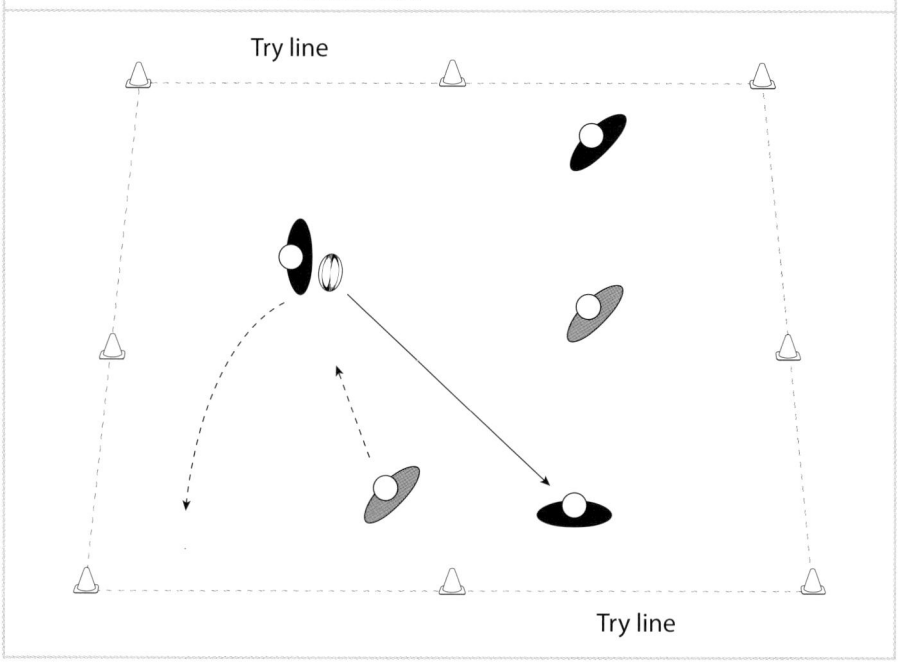

Try line

Try line

| Increase Difficulty: | • Reduce the size of the pitch
• Increase the number of defenders (2 v 3) | Decrease Difficulty: | • Increase the size of the pitch
• Increase the number of attackers (3 v 2) |

Key Coaching Points / Questions:

Passer

- Passer to have feet slight distance apart
- Ball placed lengthways in front of feet
- Knees flexed to lower the centre of gravity
- Hands to be placed either side of the ball
- Passer to drive off feet and move body weight forwards while extending hands towards the target
- Chin off chest and eyes looking at the target
- Hands to follow through and point to contact

Catcher

- Hands up ready to receive, 'W' shape in front of the chest
- Moving on balls of feet in readiness to react
- Develop vision to be able to keep an eye on the ball and the players who are free to receive a pass – chin off chest

Progression 1:

Game to continue as pass and move, with a range of passes introduced, such as dive pass, pass to the left hand side only, pass to the right hand side only and swivel pass.

Progression 2:

Game to continue as pass and move, with the player to make a decision as to when to pick up the ball from the ground and attack the try line without being touched by the opposition (one hand). Scrum-half must score or pass the ball prior to being touched, otherwise the ball is turned over. (*Note:* Receiving players must always touch the ball on the ground before continuing to pass/run.)

PRACTICE 9

Title: General handling skills	Time: 10 minutes
	Kit: Rugby ball, tennis ball, reaction ball, football, basketball, wall, rugby post
Objective: Develop catching skills and reactions	Organisation: Individual practice
Game Principles: Gaining possession	Grid Size: 5m x 5m close to wall

Description:
- Players stand close to the wall
- Throw ball against the wall, react to the bounce and move to catch the ball
- Vary the throw – high, low, soft and fast throws – to test reactions
- Practice catching the high ball and low ball with one- and two-handed catches

Relevant Positions: Back three, centre, fly-half, scrum-half, prop forward, hooker, second row, back row

Increase Difficulty:	• Stand closer to the wall to reduce reaction time • Use balls of different sizes and shapes	Decrease Difficulty:	• Use round ball only

Key Coaching Points / Questions:
- Keep eye on the ball
- Use soft hands to catch
- Throw high, low, soft and hard throws to vary catching height
- Initially catch with two hands on the ball
- Move on balls of feet in readiness to react

Progression 1:
Vary distance away from the wall – further away to introduce greater movement to the practice and closer to the wall to reduce time to correct position for the pass. Use different sizes and types of ball.

Progression 2:
Progress to one-handed catches using different sizes and types of ball.

PRACTICE 10

Title: Restarts: Catching a high ball	Time: 10 minutes
	Kit: 2 balls, cones
Objective: Develop the high-ball handling skills of the lock – catching on the ground	Organisation: Pairs
Game Principles: Gaining possession from opposition restarts	Grid Size: 10m x 10m
Description:	• In pairs, players throw the ball high in end-over-end fashion to each other
	• Vary the point the ball is thrown to ensure the player moves to the flight of the ball
	• Include moving forwards and backwards as well as sideways
Relevant Positions: Back three, centre, fly-half, scrum-half, prop forward, hooker, second row, back row	

| Increase Difficulty: | • Increase the height of the throw
• Use different types of ball (e.g. football, tennis) | Decrease Difficulty: | • Reduce the height of the throw |

Key Coaching Points / Questions:

- Head and eyes up, looking at the ball
- Move to the flight of the ball
- Hands up ready to receive the ball – can the ball be caught above the head or is a catch at chest height more appropriate?
- Turn the body to protect in contact and avoid a knock-on if the ball is dropped

Progression 1:

The thrower can advance towards the catcher and attempt to perform a 'tag-tackle' while the ball is caught. Increase or decrease the amount of pressure, depending on the levels of success. Instead of throwing the ball, it may be kicked. Once catcher is confident, an element of contact can be introduced. Start with a block-and-hold tackle, ensuring that both players remain on their feet. Develop to full-contact tackle when catcher is confident and competent.

Progression 2:

Catcher must jump to collect the ball. As above, introduce pressure on the catch by the thrower attempting to tackle the catcher.

Progression 3:

Must be supervised by an appropriately qualified coach

Only progress to a full challenge in the air once you are confident that the players can perform the skill safely.

PRACTICE 11

Title: Restarts: Jumping to catch, supported	Time: 10 minutes
	Kit: Rugby ball
Objective: Develop the high-ball handling skills of the lock – catching in the air (supported)	Organisation: Unit (jumper and supporters), Kicker
Game Principles: Gaining possession from opposition restarts	Grid Size: 10m x 10m to start – moving to pitch
Description: The jumper practises moving to the flight of the ball to receive in the air, supported by supporting players	
Relevant Positions: Prop forward, hooker, second row, back row	

Increase Difficulty:	• Decrease the time the ball is in the air	Decrease Difficulty:	• Increase the height the ball is thrown/kicked

Key Coaching Points / Questions:

Must be supervised by an appropriately qualified coach

- Head and eyes up, looking at the ball
- Move to the flight of the ball
- Turn the body to protect in contact and avoid a knock-on if the ball is dropped
- Time jump to meet the ball at the highest point of the jump
- A player in the air cannot be tackled
- Supporting players follow the movement of the catcher/jumper
- Supporting players support the catcher/jumper in the same way as in the line-out
- Catch the ball above the head – watch the ball into hands

Progression 1:

Vary the point to which the ball is thrown to ensure that the player moves to the flight of the ball. Include moving forwards and backwards as well as sideways. Supporters ensure that the jumper/catcher is supported safely in the air.

Progression 2:

The thrower can advance towards the catcher to distract them. Increase or decrease the amount of pressure, depending on the levels of success. Instead of throwing the ball, it may be kicked.

Progression 3:

Once confident and competent at catching under the pressure of distraction, an element of competition can be introduced. Start with players standing close and jumping for the ball, then increase the distance between catcher and thrower. Initially, the chasing player should be relatively passive in his challenge until the catcher becomes confident and competent. You may wish to consider the use of a contact shield to give the catcher a target to jump against.

Progression 4:

Only progress to a full challenge in the air once you are confident that the players can perform the skill safely.

RUNNING AND EVASION

Practice games in this section:

12. Truck and trailer

13. Stuck in the mud

14. 1 v 1: Change of pace, sidestep and swerve

15. Running lines

16. 2 v 2: Decision-making

THE RFU GUIDE TO COACHING POSITIONAL SKILLS

PRACTICE 12

Title: Truck and trailer *(Can also be used as a good warm-up game)*	**Time:** 10 minutes
	Kit: Balls, bibs, cones
Objective: Improve evasion skills	**Organisation:** Groups of 4–6
Game Principles: Pressure, support and continuity	**Grid Size:** 10m x 10m

Description:
- In pairs, number players 1 and 2
- Player 1 starts with the ball and must try to evade player 2
- After 1 minute the ball is swapped over

Relevant Positions: Back three, centre, fly-half, scrum-half, prop forward, hooker, second row, back row

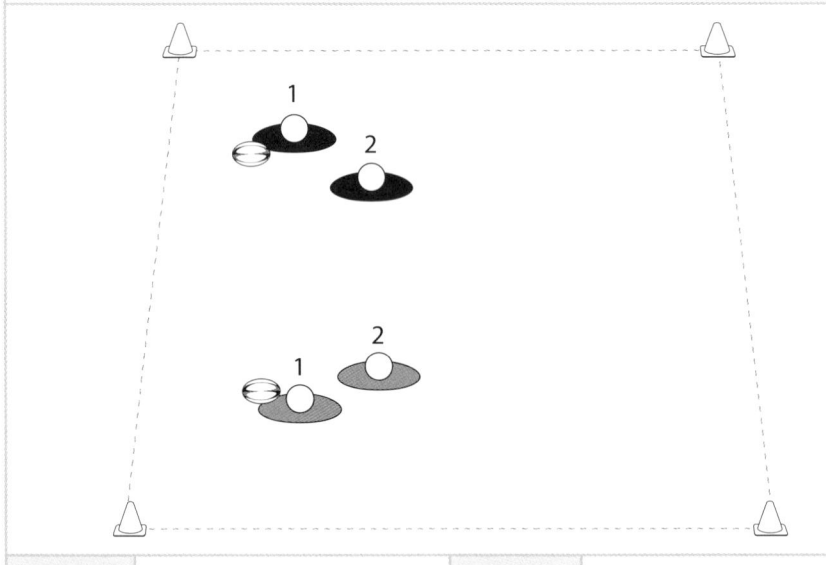

Increase Difficulty:	• Reduce the grid size • Introduce an extra ball	Decrease Difficulty:	• Increase the grid size • Condition movement of defenders

Key Coaching Points / Questions:
- Moving on balls of feet in readiness to react
- Stay balanced using small steps
- Try different evasive moves: swerves, acceleration, sidesteps etc.

Progression:
Reduce the size of the grid to reduce the space available for movement.

68

PRACTICE 13

Title: Stuck in the mud *(Can also be used as a good warm-up game)*	Time: 10 minutes
	Kit: Balls, bibs, cones
Objective: Improve basic core handling skills	Organisation: Groups of 4–6
Game Principles: Pressure, support and continuity	Grid Size: 10m x 10m

Description:
- Ball carrier tries to catch members of the opposing team by touching them with the ball
- Once caught, opposing player must stand with arms out, in line with shoulders
- Opposing players can be freed by their own team running under their raised arms
- Swap players once all players have been caught or after 2 minutes, whichever is sooner

Relevant Positions: Back three, centre, fly-half, scrum-half, prop forward, hooker, second row, back row

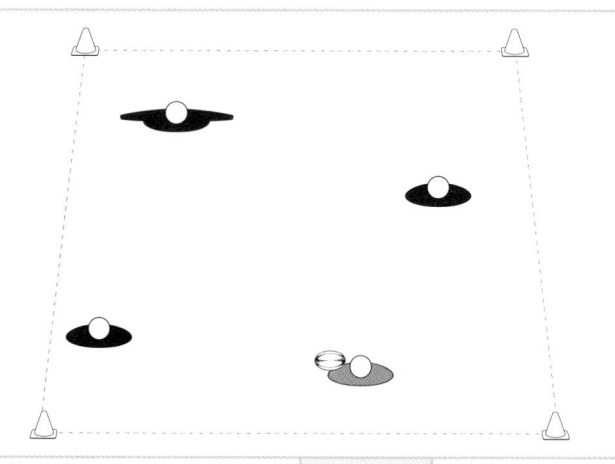

Increase Difficulty:	• Reduce the grid size • Introduce an extra ball	Decrease Difficulty:	• Increase the grid size • Condition movement of defenders

Key Coaching Points / Questions:
- Moving on balls of feet in readiness to react
- Stay balanced using small steps
- Try different evasive moves: swerves, acceleration, sidesteps etc.

Progression:
Add extra attackers, but still one ball. Only the ball carrier can catch opposition, but may pass the ball.

PRACTICE 14

Title: 1 v 1: Change of pace, sidestep and swerve	Time: 10–15 minutes
	Kit: 1 ball, cones
Objective: Develop running skills and agility to beat a defender	Organisation: Pairs
Game Principles: Go forwards	Grid Size: 10m x 5m

Description:
- Attacker stands at one end of the grid and is fed ball by the defender
- Attacker looks to make best use of space to beat the defender and score a try at the end of the grid

Relevant Positions: Back three, centre, fly-half, scrum-half, prop forward, hooker, second row, back row

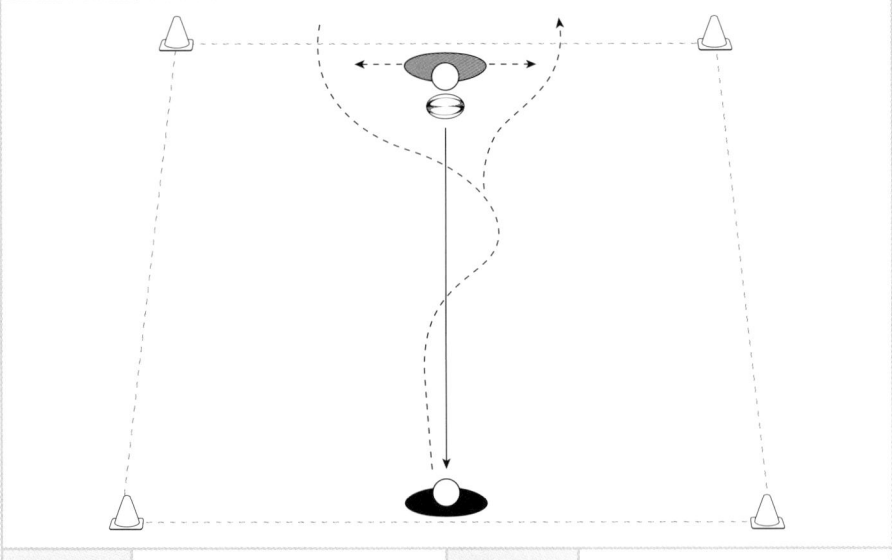

Increase Difficulty:	• Vary feed to the player • Move defender towards fly-half • Increase levels of contact defence	Decrease Difficulty:	• Limit speed and movement of defender (have them start on knees/front) • Touch tackles only

Key Coaching Points / Questions:
- Players stay balanced and on balls of feet
- Hands up and ready to receive the ball
- Chin off chest to view defender and space
- Acceleration and commitment to the running line
- Change of running line: inside to outside shoulder
- Ask player to consider ways of beating the defender

Progression 1:

Change of pace

- Run at less than full pace with shortened stride
- Prior to the tackle increase to full pace
- Accelerate away from defender

Progression 2:

Use of sidestep

- Carry the ball in two hands

If the defender is coming from the left:

- Shorten stride for balance and timing
- Transfer weight onto the right foot over a bent right knee to keep the defender on the same running path
- Drive hard off the right foot and accelerate away to the left against the running path of the defender
- Transfer the ball across the body away from the defender

Progression 3:

The swerve

- Run at speed at the defender's inside shoulder
- Carry the ball in two hands
- Using upper body, feint to go one way
- As the defender checks, swing hips round and away from the defender in the opposite direction
- Accelerate away in an arc around the defender

PRACTICE 15

Title: Running lines	Time: 5–10 minutes
	Kit: 1 ball, cones
Objective: Develop the running lines of a player	Organisation: Groups of 3 or 5
Game Principles: Go forwards	Grid Size: 10m x 10m
Description: • Player stands at the bottom of the grid and moves forwards on to a pass made from the side of the grid • Ball carrier decides on running line based on the position of the defence • Player may decide to change running line after receipt of the ball in order to beat the defender	
Relevant Positions: Back three, centre, fly-half, scrum-half, prop forward, hooker, second row, back row	

Increase Difficulty:	• Vary depth and width of pass • Play from both sides • Introduce defence • Vary the style of pass	Decrease Difficulty:	• Without opposition • Short passes to start • Walk/jog through

Key Coaching Points / Questions:
- Hands up and across the body towards the ball
- Emphasise the outside arm across the body – this will help turn hips towards the ball and open up the body for receipt of the pass
- 'W' shape with the hands (palms facing towards the ball, thumbs touching, fingers pointing up)
- Elbows tight to the body
- Clear call for the pass
- Sight ball and opposition early to establish running line
- Consider deception of defence through running line and body movement
- Acceleration and commitment to the running line

Progression 1:
Vary style of pass. Vary depth and width of pass.

Progression 2:
Develop a change in angle of run for the ball carrier: consideration to be given to running on the inside/outside shoulder of the defender. A straight line can also be effective when support is added.

Progression 3:
Introduce an additional defender. Ball carrier to react to defensive pattern and run at space.

Progression 4:
Introduce support for the ball carrier so he has an option either side. A change of pace/deceleration should be encouraged to hold the defence, for support to run at space.

PRACTICE 16A

Title: 2 v 2: Decision-making	**Time:** 10–15 minutes
	Kit: 1 ball, cones
Objective: Develop decision-making of player to wrong-foot the defence and attack space between or outside two defenders	**Organisation:** Groups of 4
Game Principles: Go forwards and support	**Grid Size:** 10m x 10m
Description: • Ball carrier and support player stand at one end of the grid and are fed a ball from two defenders • On receipt of the ball, the player (ball carrier) and support player move to wrong-foot and attack space either side of defenders.	

Relevant Positions: Back three, centre, fly-half, scrum-half, prop forward, hooker, second row, back row

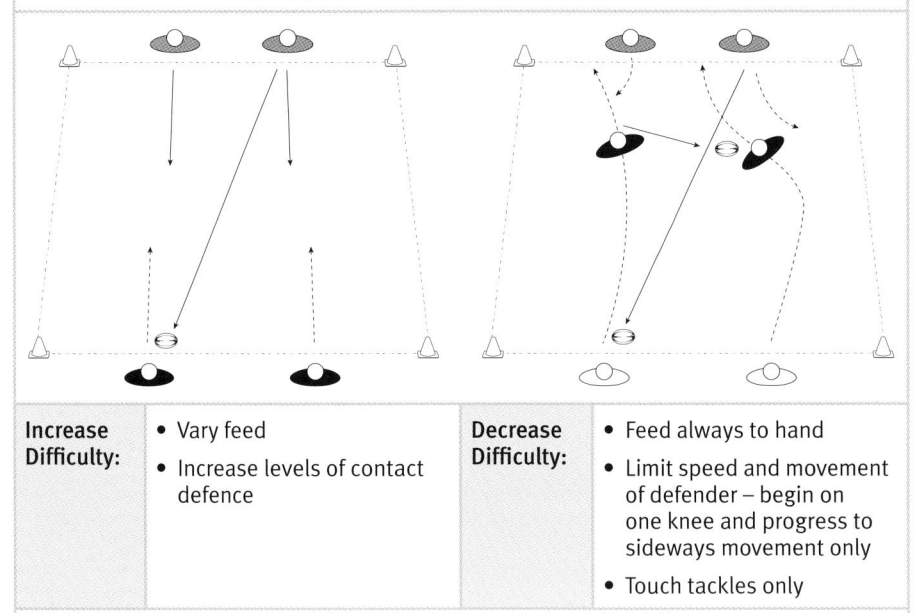

Increase Difficulty:	• Vary feed • Increase levels of contact defence	Decrease Difficulty:	• Feed always to hand • Limit speed and movement of defender – begin on one knee and progress to sideways movement only • Touch tackles only

Key Coaching Points / Questions:

Attacking space between defenders

- Ball carrier and support player have hands up and ready to receive the ball
- Head up to view defender and space
- Ball carrier to run on inside shoulder of first defender to move to the side of the grid
- Support player to run at outside shoulder of second defender and move them to outside of the grid
- Support player changes running line or sidesteps to run on inside shoulder and attack space between defenders
- Ball carrier pops the ball into the space between the defenders for support player to attack
- Ball carrier to have elbows tight to the body and use fingers and wrists to adjust pop pass for runner
- Consider range of passes and accuracy of pass to reflect run of support player

PRACTICE 16B

Title: 2 v 2: Decision-making

Time: 10–15 minutes

Kit: Ball, cones

Description: As 16A

Key Coaching Points / Questions:

Attacking space outside of defenders

- Ball carrier and support player have hands up and ready to receive the ball
- Head up to view defender and space
- Ball carrier to run straight at the first defender and decelerate to keep defender in position
- Support player to run at inside shoulder of second defender and move him to inside/middle of the grid
- Support player changes running line or sidesteps to run on outside shoulder and attack space preserved on the outside of the defender/grid
- Ball carrier passes the ball into the space for support player to attack
- Ball carrier to have firm wrists to play a long pass into the path of support player
- Hands and arms to follow through pass and point to the target

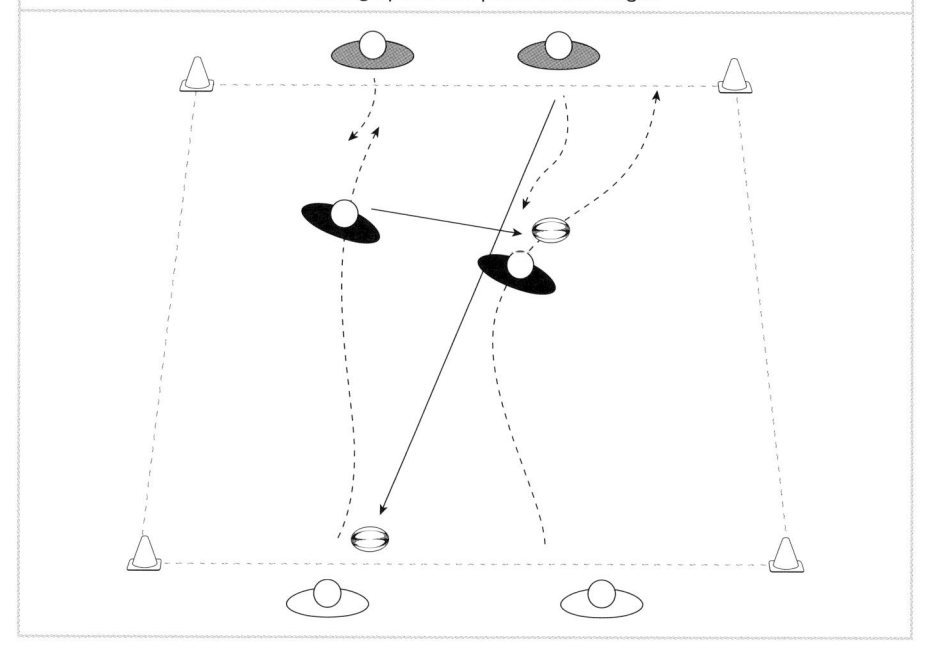

PRACTICE 16C

Title: 2 v 2: Decision-making

Time: 10–15 minutes

Kit: Ball, cones

Description: As 16A

Key Coaching Points / Questions:

Wrong-foot the defence using a switch

- Ball carrier and support player have hands up and ready to receive the ball
- Head up to view defender and space
- Both ball carrier and support player run straight lines to hold the running line of the opposing defenders
- On the call of 'Switch!', players change direction and run diagonally towards support player
- Ball carrier 'lifts' the ball into the pathway of support player, who continues diagonal line until he is on the outside shoulder of defender. At this point he straightens his running line
- Ball carrier to allow some hang time on the ball
- Ball carrier to ensure he has moved initial defender with him to make sure gap is created for support to attack

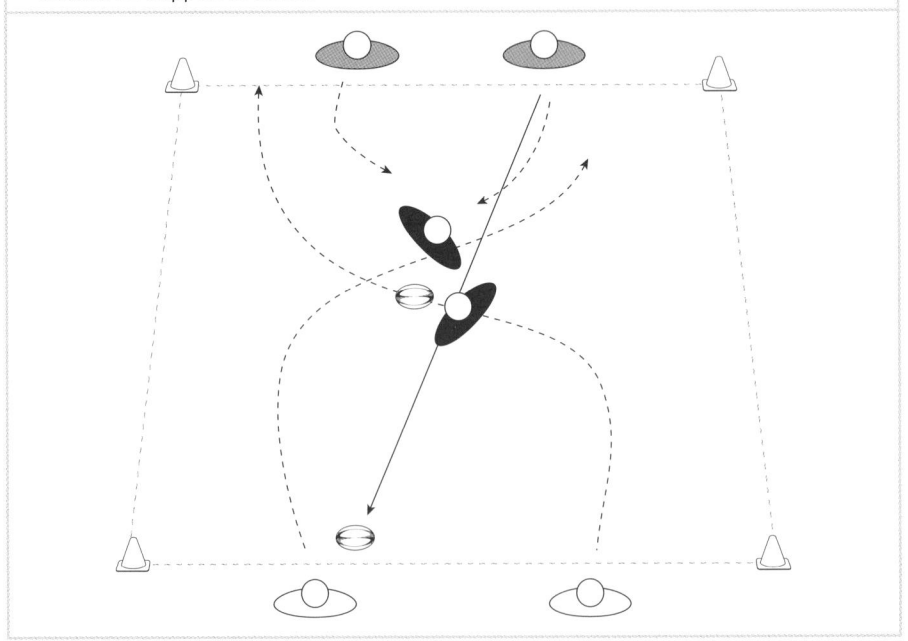

PRACTICE 16D

Title: 2 v 2: Decision-making	Time: 10–15 minutes
	Kit: Ball, cones

Description: As 16A

Key Coaching Points / Questions:

Wrong-foot the defence to create an overlap with a loop

- Ball carrier runs a straight line at opposition defender
- Prior to making pass to support, ball carrier changes direction towards support player
- Support player runs at the inside shoulder of the opposing defender and draws him into the centre of the grid
- Support player receives a pass and continues to move forwards to interest outside defender
- Player who started as ball carrier, now without the ball, becomes the 'looping player' and loops around the outside of the former support player (now the ball carrier) to offer a passing option
- Looping player must gain ground while running an arc
- Looping player straightens outside support player and receives pass in the area of the grid that is not defended
- Pass from the new ball carrier player is flat
- The new ball carrier may need to decelerate prior to pass to provide more time to execute and to hold defender in position. Ball carrier to ensure he has moved initial defender with him to make sure gap is created for support to attack

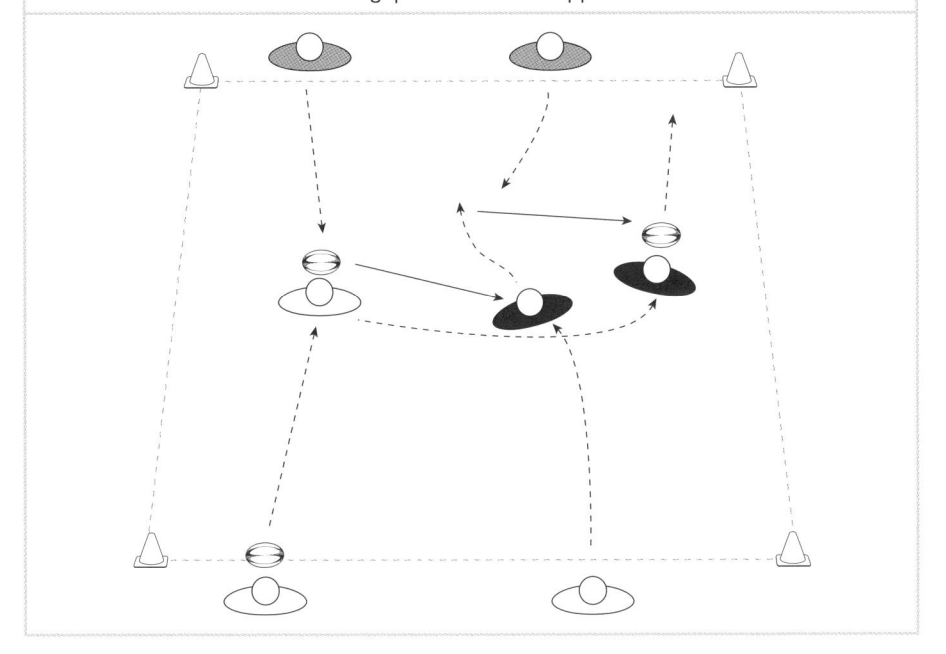

CONTINUITY

Practice games in this section:

17. Beating the first defender using support

18. Contesting possession on the floor (the ruck)

PRACTICE 17A

Title: Beating the first defender using support

Time: 5–10 minutes

Kit: 1 ball, cones

Objective: Develop skills to move first defender and create advantage from the contact

Organisation: Groups of 3 or 5

Game Principles: Apply pressure, support, compete for possession, decision-making and hierarchy of contact

Grid Size: 10m x 5m

Description:
- First player receives pass from the side of the grid and becomes the ball carrier
- Ball carrier attacks the defender and uses one-on-one skills to either beat defender or move him to create space and use support options
- Support player reacts to the movement of the ball carrier and looks to support or exploit space depending on the outcome of the contact

Relevant Positions: Back three, centre, fly-half, scrum-half, prop forward, hooker, second row, back row

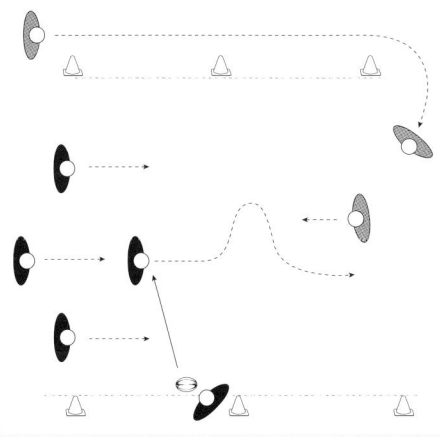

Increase Difficulty:	• Progress from static defender to defender moving towards ball carrier • Increase levels of contact defence	Decrease Difficulty:	• Limit speed and movement of defender – begin on one knee and progress to sideways movement only • Touch tackles only

Key Coaching Points / Questions:

Must be supervised by an appropriately qualified coach

Ball carrier passes before contact

- Ball carrier moves defender to create space using change of pace, running line, sidestep or swerve
- Support player moves to exploit space and communicates position
- Ball carrier is aware of support options and passes ball before contact
- Use of fingers and wrists to offload the ball to support

Progression 1:

Defenders to move forwards and apply pressure.

Progression 2:

Work with support players to develop running lines that will provide space to attack.

Progression 3:

Add further defenders so that attackers have to beat two defenders.

SMALL-SIDED GAMES

PRACTICE 17B

Title: Beating the first defender using support   **Time:** 5–10 minutes

Kit: Ball, cones

Description: 17A

Key Coaching Points / Questions:

Must be supervised by an appropriately qualified coach

Ball carrier passes during or after contact/tackle

- Ball carrier uses foot movement before contact to put defender off balance
- Ball carrier takes contact, aiming at the weak edges (arms and shoulders) of the defender, choosing not to hit the strong core of the defender
- Support player reads the situation and decides on the best line of run to accept the offload pass
- Support player keeps depth, communicates position to the ball carrier and times run to receive the offload pass
- Support player accelerates past the defender

Progression 1:

Defenders to move forwards and apply pressure to the ball carrier.

Progression 2:

Work with support players to recognise the best running lines and when to begin supporting run to gain most advantage.

Progression 3:

Add further defenders so that attackers have to beat two defenders.

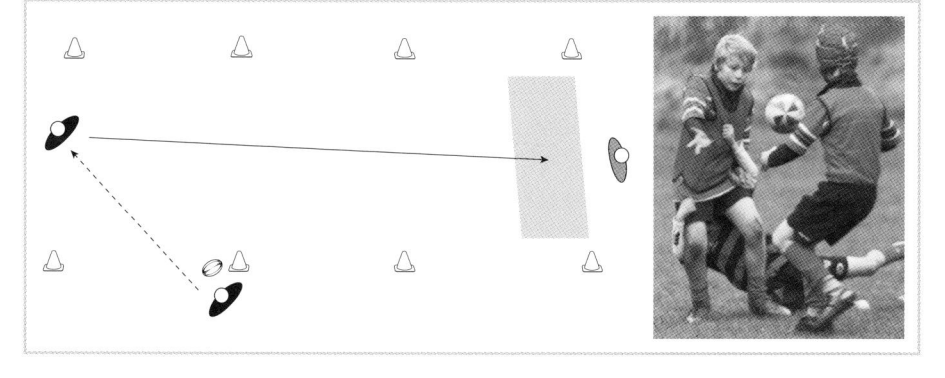

81

THE RFU GUIDE TO COACHING POSITIONAL SKILLS

PRACTICE 17C

Title: Beating the first defender using support

Time: 5–10 minutes

Kit: Ball, cones

Description: As 17A

Key Coaching Points / Questions:

Must be supervised by an appropriately qualified coach

Support player secures and rips ball from ball carrier in contact, and either offloads or rolls past the defender

- Ball carrier uses foot movement before contact to put defender off balance
- Ball carrier takes contact, aiming at the weak edges (arms and shoulders) of the defender, choosing not to hit the strong core of the defender
- Support player reads the situation and goes into contact with the ball carrier, secures the ball and rips the ball away from the defender
- Support player (now the ball carrier) rolls out of contact and either offloads to a second support runner or rolls and accelerates past the defender

Progression 1:

Defenders to move forwards and apply pressure to the ball carrier.

Progression 2:

Work with support players to recognise the best running lines and when to begin supporting run to gain most advantage.

Progression 3:

Add further defenders so that attackers have to beat two defenders.

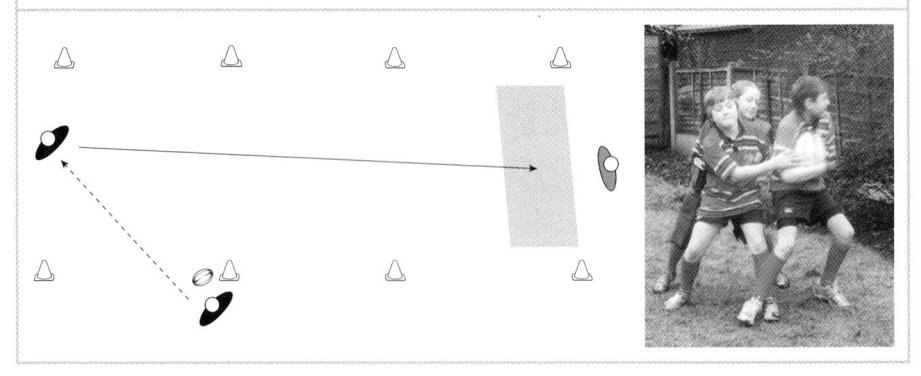

PRACTICE 17D

Title: Beating the first defender using support   **Time:** 5–10 minutes

Kit: Ball, cones

Description: As 17A

Key Coaching Points / Questions:

Must be supervised by an appropriately qualified coach

Support player latches onto ball carrier in contact and drives to make ground

- Ball carrier uses foot movement before contact to put defender off balance
- Ball carrier takes contact, aiming at the weak edges (arms and shoulders) of the defender
- Support player reads the situation and decides best option is to latch onto ball carrier and drive forwards (this is generally the case if the ball carrier still has forward momentum or has taken contact in a forwards-facing position)
- Support player binds onto ball carrier and helps to keep ball carrier in a forwards-facing direction
- Ball carrier and support player both drive to gain ground

Progression 1:

Defenders to move forwards and apply pressure to the ball carrier.

Progression 2:

Work with support players to recognise the best supporting action.

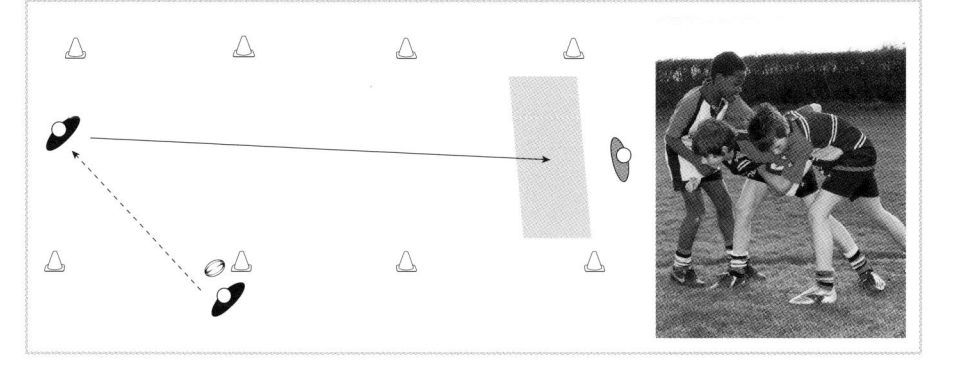

THE RFU GUIDE TO COACHING POSITIONAL SKILLS

PRACTICE 17E

Title: Beating the first defender using support **Time:** 5–10 minutes

Kit: Ball, cones

Description: As 17A

Key Coaching Points / Questions:

Must be supervised by an appropriately qualified coach

Support player secures ball and sets up a maul

- Ball carrier uses foot movement before contact to put defender off balance
- Ball carrier takes contact, aiming at the weak edges (arms and shoulders) of the defender, choosing not to hit the strong core of the defender
- Support player reads the situation and decides best option is to secure the ball and create a maul position
- Support player secures ball and moves it away from the defender, keeping it securely held
- Ball carrier and support player both drive to gain ground

Progression 1:

Defenders to move forwards and apply pressure to the ball carrier.

Progression 2:

Ball carrier and support players to experiment with different ways of keeping the ball available and taking the most effective supporting actions.

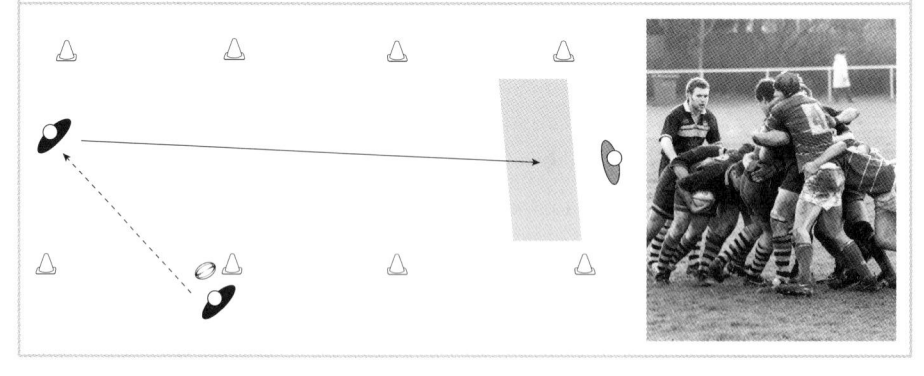

PRACTICE 17F

Title: Beating the first defender using support

Time: 5–10 minutes

Kit: Ball, cones

Description: As 17A

Key Coaching Points / Questions:

Must be supervised by an appropriately qualified coach

Ball carrier takes contact and sets up ruck

- Ball carrier uses foot movement before contact to put defender off balance
- Ball carrier takes contact, aiming at the weak edges (arms and shoulders) of the defender, choosing not to hit the strong core of the defender
- Ball carrier goes to ground and makes the decision to either:
  a) Pop pass off the ground to a supporting player, or
  b) Place the ball on the ground in a position to benefit the attacking players
- Ball carrier must release the ball after contact with the ground

Progression 1:

Encourage support player to look for signals indicating the ball carrier's intentions (i.e. pop pass or place the ball) and take one of the following appropriate actions:

- Take the pop pass from the ball carrier and use available space
- Pick the ball off the floor and accelerate past defender
- Take contact with the defender and form a ruck.

Progression 2:

Add extra defender(s) and explore how the positioning of defenders affects the support decision. For example:

- If defenders are close to the ball, forming a ruck may be the best option.
- If defence are scattered, then the pick and drive may be effective.

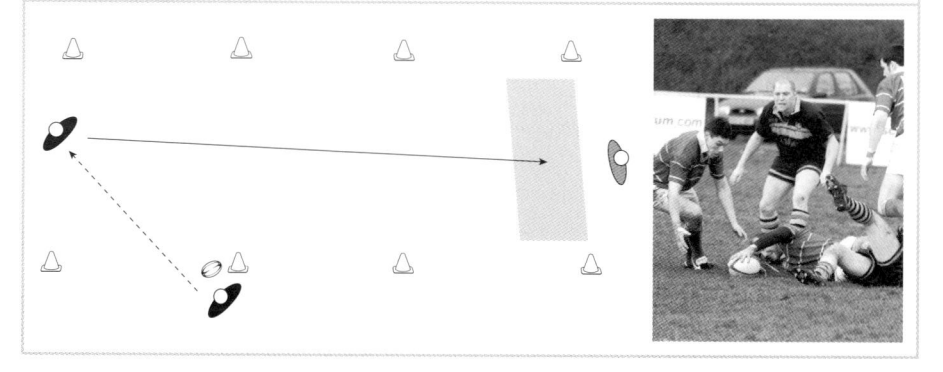

PRACTICE 18

Title: Contesting possession on the floor (the ruck)	**Time:** 30 minutes
	Kit: Balls, cones, tackle suits (optional)
Objective: Improve basic core handling skills	**Organisation:** Groups of 2 or 4
Game Principles: Apply pressure, support, compete for possession, and decision-making	**Grid Size:** 5m x 5m

Description:
- Two players lie face down on the ground, aligned in the same direction
- Coach feeds ball between the players and they have to battle for the ball on the ground
- Player winning the ball places the ball as if to set up a ruck
- Encourage player who has lost the ball to get onto his feet quickly and contest for the ball

Relevant Positions: Back three, centre, fly-half, scrum-half, prop forward, hooker, second row, back row

Increase Difficulty:	• Encourage ball winner to try different placements for the ball: a Close to body b As far as possible from defender • Increase pressure on defender to contest for the ball	**Decrease Difficulty:**	• Condition game to allow one player to win the ball

Key Coaching Points / Questions:

Ball winner
- Work hard to win the ball
- Call 'Ball won!'
- Turn to position ball to help your support players
- Place ball to avoid the ball rolling around
- Experiment with different body positions to make it difficult for opponent to compete for the ball

Player without the ball (opponent)
- Call 'Ball lost!'
- Work hard to get onto feet quickly
- Challenge for the ball

Progression:

Progress to four players, two on each side. Coach feeds ball between the two central players. When the ball is won by one side the ball winner communicates that the ball is won. The support player on the winning side quickly gets into position to protect the ball. The two players on the losing team compete for the ball. A ruck is formed and all players must keep shoulders above hips and drive to win the ball.

KICKING

Practice games in this section:

19. The punt

20. Rugby netball – kicking

21. The grubber

22. Grubber kick goals

23. The drop kick

24. The box kick

PRACTICE 19

Title: The punt	Time: 10 minutes
	Kit: Ball
Objective: Apply pressure by gaining field position or relieving pressure with a kick into touch	Organisation: Groups of 2 or 3
Game Principles: Go forwards and pressure	Grid Size: 10m x 30m

Description:
- Players face each other in the grid
- Kicker practises technique for the punt kick
- Begin over a small area to develop technique and accuracy, then extend kicking distance

Relevant Positions: Back three, centre, fly-half, scrum-half

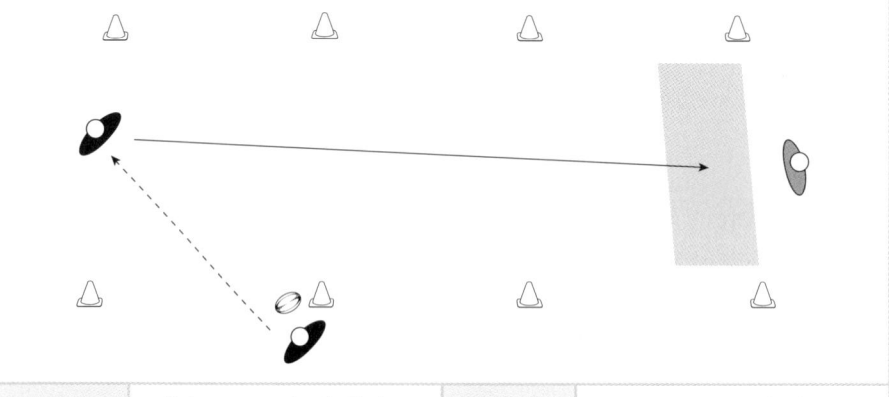

Increase Difficulty:	• Kicker to receive ball via varied feed • Partner to apply pressure by following up feed	Decrease Difficulty:	• No pressure applied

Key Coaching Points / Questions:
- Head and shoulders should be still
- Ball pointed in the direction of the intended kick
- Eyes on the ball
- Ball held in two hands and dropped onto the laces of the boot
- Extended leg on contact
- Point toe on contact and keep head over the ball
- Kick through the widest part of the ball
- Keep the kicking leg straight while swinging through the ball
- Follow through with the kicking leg and opposite arm for balance

Progression 1:
Vary feed to partner so that he has to adjust body position prior to kicking to target area.

Progression 2:
Feeder to apply pressure to kick by acting as a defender – jogging prior to running.

PRACTICE 20

Title: Rugby netball – kicking	**Time:** 10 minutes
	Kit: Balls, bibs, cones
Objective: Achieve line penetration using a punt kick into space behind opposition for own team to regather	**Organisation:** Groups of 6
Game Principles: Kicking into space	**Grid Size:** 30m x 30m

Description:
- Split into two teams of three players and assign try lines at opposite ends of the grid
- Ball starts in the middle
- No players are allowed within 2m of the ball carrier
- Players are not allowed to move with the ball
- Ball is passed using a punt kick
- If ball is dropped, possession is turned over
- Try is scored in normal fashion
- After each try, play restarts from where try is scored

Relevant Positions: Back three, centre, fly-half, scrum-half

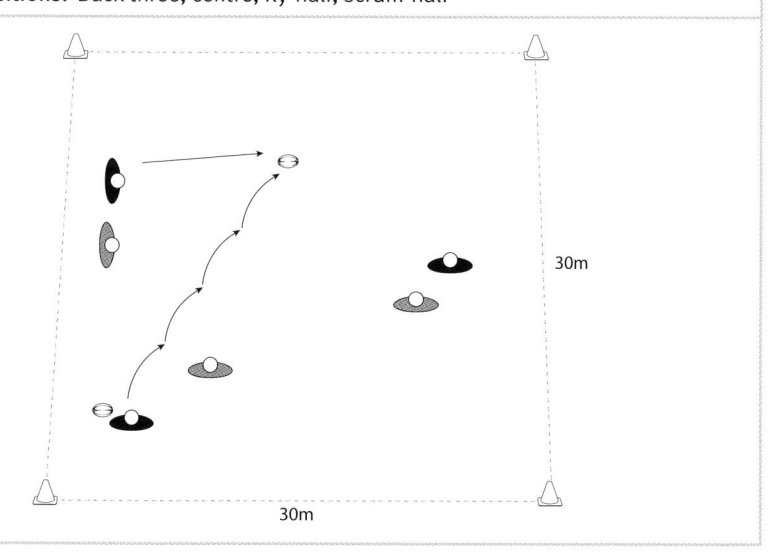

Increase Difficulty:	• Reduce size of the grid • Add another ball	Decrease Difficulty:	• Increase size of grid • Reduce number of defenders

Key Coaching Points / Questions:

Game key points

- Kick into space for teammate to run on to
- Quick footwork in order to vary target of kick
- Non-ball-carrying attackers communicate presence of space
- Defenders man mark

Grubber kick key points

- Two hands on ball
- Point ball down towards the ground
- Kick ball into the ground with knee over ball
- Keep body in line and pointing towards target
- Keep body over the ball to keep the ball down
- Use straight follow through to create extra power

Progression 1:
Use grubber kicks instead of punt kicks to improve accuracy of chip kick.

Progression 2:
Allow movement with the ball: three steps, then movement until touched.

PRACTICE 21

Title: The grubber	**Time:** 10 minutes
	Kit: Ball
Objective: Apply pressure by putting the ball through and behind defences for attacking side to chase and regain possession; find touch outside of the 22	**Organisation:** Groups of 2 or 3
Game Principles: Go forwards and pressure	**Grid Size:** 10m x 30m
Description: • Players face each other in the grid • Kicker practises technique for the grubber kick • Begin over a small area to develop technique and accuracy, then extend kicking distance	
Relevant Positions: Back three, centre, fly-half, scrum-half	

SMALL-SIDED GAMES

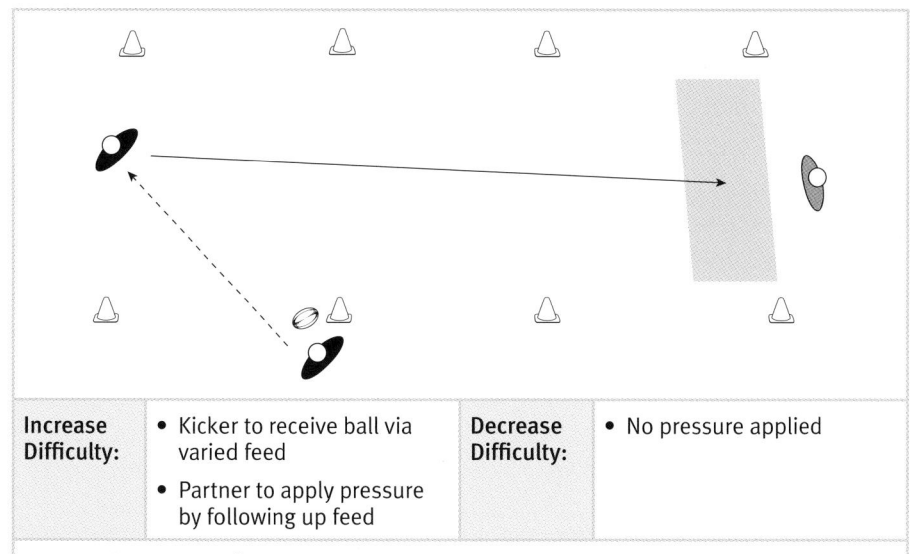

Increase Difficulty:	• Kicker to receive ball via varied feed • Partner to apply pressure by following up feed	Decrease Difficulty:	• No pressure applied

Key Coaching Points / Questions:

Game key points

- Head and shoulders still
- Ball held in two hands and so that the axis is in line with the foot
- Tilt the ball backwards slightly, towards the body
- Eyes on the ball
- Drop ball onto laces of the boot
- Point toe on contact and keep head over the ball
- Keep knee slightly ahead of the ball
- Kick through the top of the ball
- Keep the kicking leg straight while swinging through the ball
- Kick ball along the ground

Progression 1:

Vary feed to partner so that he has to adjust body position prior to kicking to target area.

Progression 2:

Feeder to apply pressure to kick by acting as a defender – jogging prior to running.

91

PRACTICE 22

Title: Grubber kick goals	Time: 10 minutes
	Kit: Ball, cones
Objective: Improve the ability to identify space for a grubber kick and improve accuracy of kick	Organisation: Groups of 3–6
Game Principles: Kicking to space	Grid Size: N/A

Description:
- Gate sizes and distances between gates can vary as accuracy improves
- Ball carrier must kick the ball through gates (between cones)
- Ball carrier is not allowed out of shaded area
- Defenders must not enter shaded area
- Defenders must try to stop the ball carrier grubber kicking the ball through any of the gates
- Once the ball is kicked through a gate, the ball is returned to the attacker and play continues
- After 2 minutes, players rotate roles

Relevant Positions: Back three, centre, fly-half, scrum-half

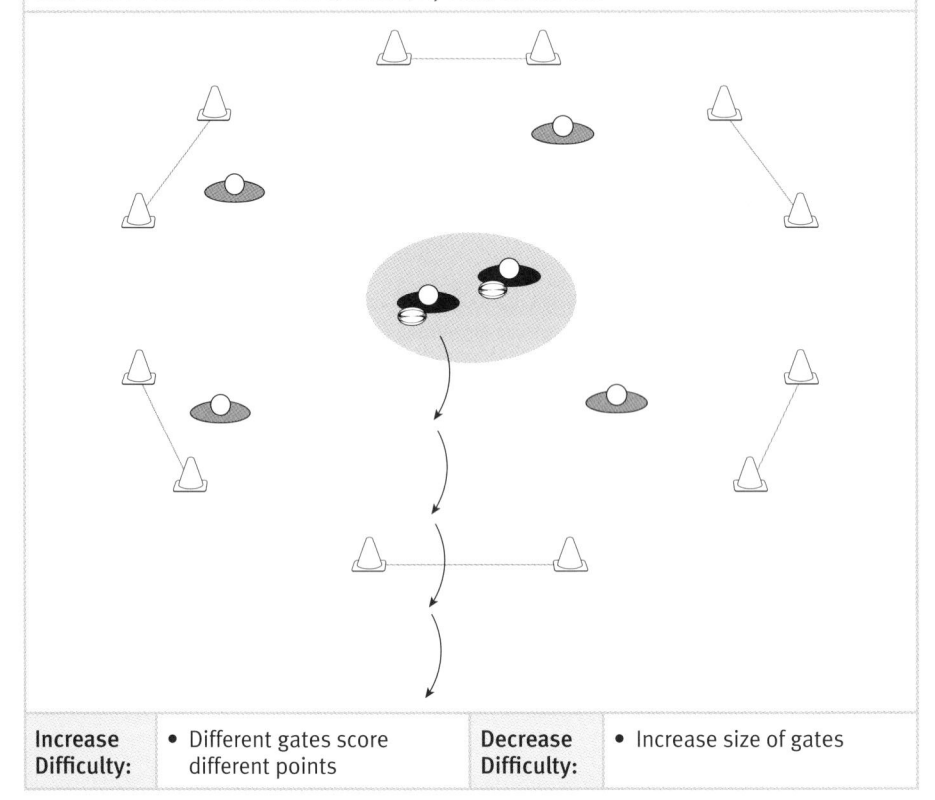

Increase Difficulty:	• Different gates score different points	Decrease Difficulty:	• Increase size of gates

Key Coaching Points / Questions:

Game key points
- Stay on toes in order to reposition quickly
- Dummy kick to commit defenders to a gate
- Use improvisation in order to achieve success

Grubber kick key points
- Two hands on ball
- Ball pointing down towards the ground
- Kick ball into the ground with knee over ball
- Keep body in line and pointing towards target
- Keep body over the ball to keep the ball down
- Use straight follow through to create extra power

Progression 1:
Different gates score different points, thereby prioritising specific gates.

Progression 2:
Start defenders in the gates and remove the shaded area, replacing it with a single cone that attackers must start from. Defenders may charge down or make touch resulting in play restarting.

PRACTICE 23

Title: The drop kick	Time: 10 minutes
	Kit: Ball
Objective: Score points within the field of play or restart the game at halfway and the 22	Organisation: Groups of 2 or 3
Game Principles: Go forwards and pressure	Grid Size: 10m x 30m

Description:
- Players face each other in the grid
- Kicker practises technique for the drop kick
- Begin over a small area to develop technique and accuracy, then extend kicking distance

Relevant Positions: Back three, centre, fly-half, scrum-half

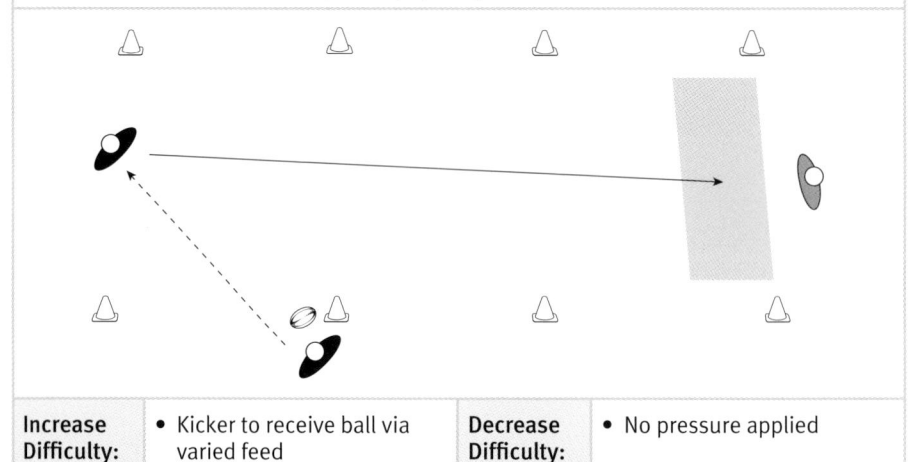

Increase Difficulty:	• Kicker to receive ball via varied feed • Partner to apply pressure by following up feed	Decrease Difficulty:	• No pressure applied

Key Coaching Points / Questions:
- Head and shoulders should be still
- Ball held in two hands and so that the point is facing the floor
- Tilt the ball backwards slightly, towards the body
- Eyes on the ball
- Head over the ball
- Drop ball directly onto its point, and slightly in front of the kicking foot
- Kick through the line of the ball, making contact on the half volley
- Follow through with the kicking leg and opposite arm for balance
- Lift toes slightly on the kick to achieve height
- Point toes on contact to generate more distance

SMALL-SIDED GAMES

Progression 1:
Vary feed to partner so that he has to adjust body position prior to kicking to target area.

Progression 2:
Feeder to apply pressure to kick by acting as a defender – jogging prior to running.

PRACTICE 24

Title: The box kick	**Time:** 15 minutes
	Kit: 4 balls, cones
Objective: Develop player's ability to apply/relieve pressure using a kick from static play	**Organisation:** Groups of 4 or 6
Game Principles: Go forwards, support and pressure	**Grid Size:** 30m x 40m
Description: • This practice is to simulate a scrum-half kicking for position from a behind breakdown or restart. • Scrum-half should identify the area of the field to kick into, to apply maximum pressure to the opposition (the box). • Scrum-half performs a kick into the box (box kick) which becomes the target for supporting players.	
Relevant Positions: Back three, centre, fly-half, scrum-half	

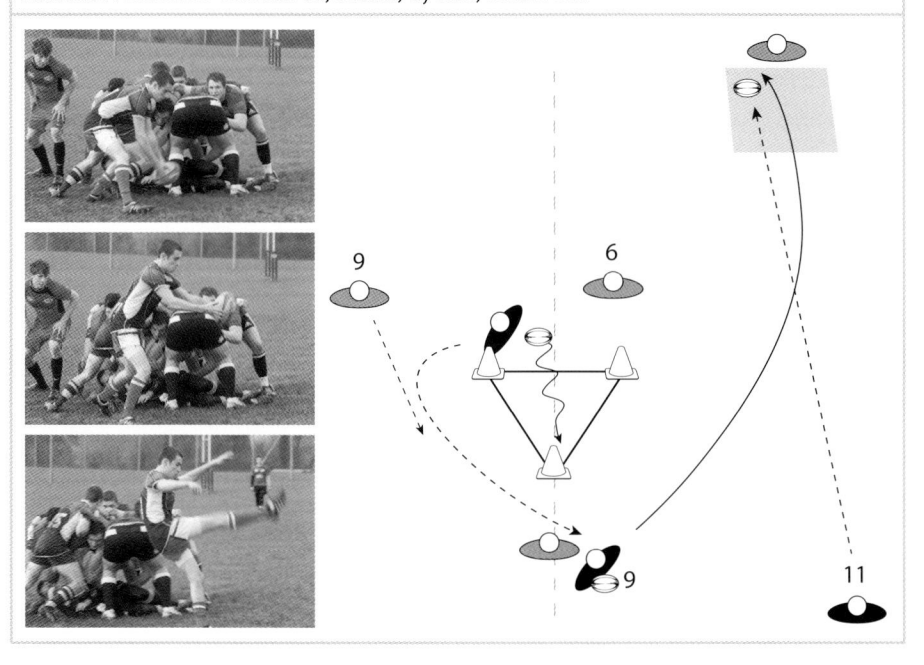

95

Increase Difficulty:	• Work on height and distance of kick for chasers • Add opposition gradually	Decrease Difficulty:	• Begin with ball in hands • Mark with cones the steps to be taken with the feed • Mark target area with cones

Key Coaching Points / Questions:
- Scrum-half to position non-kicking foot close to the ball
- Create a good base with the feet
- Rotate hips to 45-degree angle
- Pick up the ball and step away from the gain line with the non-kicking foot
- Place ball over the kicking foot and swing the kicking foot through the ball, making contact with the laces of the boot, with toes pointed
- Aim to give the ball a hang-time of 3–4 seconds in the air
- The ball should aim to land at the same point and time as the chasing players

Progression 1:
Work on finding optimum height and distance for the kick to give supporting players time to chase and compete for the ball. Add opponent to catch the ball.

Key Coaching Points / Questions:
- Accuracy of the kick
- Kick across the body
- Kick for the target areas on the pitch
- Follow through the kick

Progression 2:
Add opposition around the breakdown to put pressure on the kicking scrum-half by reducing time to kick and attempting to 'charge-down' the kick.

Key Coaching Points / Questions:
- As above

TACKLING

Practice games in this section:

25. Tackling

26. Turtle grid

27. Repetitive tackle drill

SMALL-SIDED GAMES

PRACTICE 25

Title: Tackling	Time: 15 minutes
	Kit: Balls, cones
Objective: Work in a smaller area and improve ability of players to tackle in a 1 v 1 situation	Organisation: Pairs
Game Principles: Tackle, go forwards, contest possession and apply pressure	Grid Size: 8m x 8m

Description:
- One attacker and one defender start at the same point, attacker with the ball
- Start point can be offset closer to cone 'A' to favour the attacker, or closer to point 'D' to favour defenders
- Attackers run round cone 'A' and realign to attack try line 'C–D'
- Defender runs round cone 'D' and turns to defend try line 'C–D'
- Defender attempts to tackle or play the attacker into touch before the attacker can score
- The game is over when either a try is scored, or the player is tackled or goes into touch
- Players return to the start point and the exercise is repeated

Relevant Positions: Back three, centre, fly-half, scrum-half, prop forward, hooker, second row, back row

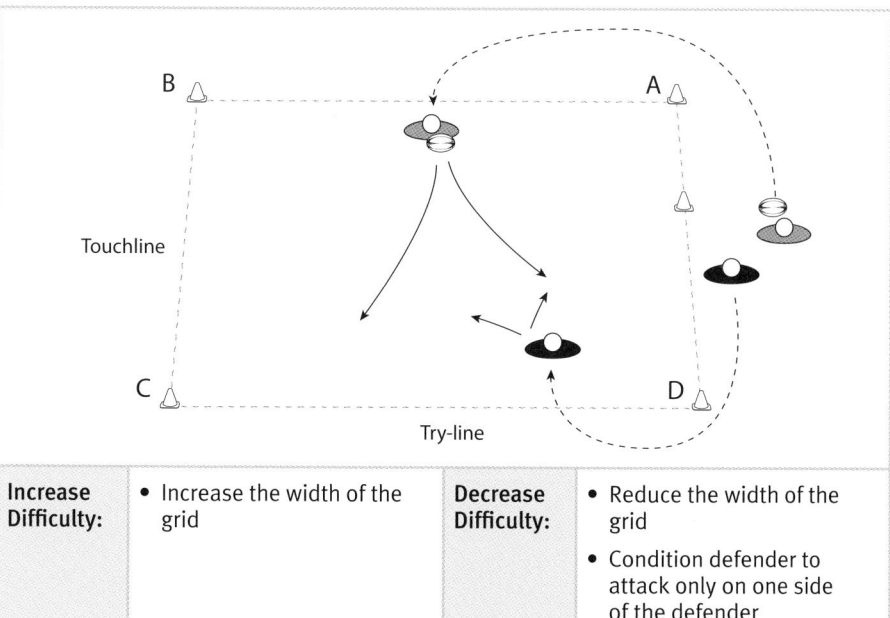

Increase Difficulty:	• Increase the width of the grid	Decrease Difficulty:	• Reduce the width of the grid
			• Condition defender to attack only on one side of the defender

97

Key Coaching Points / Questions:

Must be supervised by an appropriately qualified coach

Defender

- Watch the ball carrier, keep head up and adopt a strong athletic position, with flat back and weight forward
- Move on toes
- Keep shoulders braced and chin off chest
- Defender to make contact with his shoulder between the attacker's thigh and waist, and head behind the legs
- Wrap arms around thighs, and pull and hold tight
- Keep eyes open and drive through the ball carrier using legs
- Turn the ball carrier sideways and try to land on top of him
- Keep feet close to ball carrier in the tackle
- Tackler to get to feet immediately and contest for the ball

Progression 1:

Note: Be safety conscious at all times with tackling practice. Start with attacker and defender walking, or possibly on knees, to perfect tackle technique before progressing to running contact.

Progression 2:

Condition ball carrier to attack only one side of the defender, to simplify tackling setup.

Progression 3:

Introduce player to support ball carrier. Ball carrier can offload during or after the tackle. Work on tackler getting to feet quickly and challenging for the ball, to reduce time for the offload.

SMALL-SIDED GAMES

PRACTICE 26

Title: Turtle grid *(Can also be used as a good contact warm-up game)*	Time: 10 minutes
	Kit: Balls, bibs, cones
Objective: Improve the ability to turn a tackled player on his back into a position where the ball can easily be turned over, getting quickly to feet in order to make another turnover tackle	Organisation: Groups of 6
Game Principles: Pressure and tackling	Grid Size: 10m x 10m

Description:
- Ball carriers avoid getting tackled in the grid
- Tacklers tackle ball carriers
- Tacklers strip the ball within the laws of rugby
- Once stripped of possession, ball is handed back to the attackers and play continues
- Roles rotate after 2 minutes
- When used as a warm-up, develop from touch tackle to holding tackle to wrestle

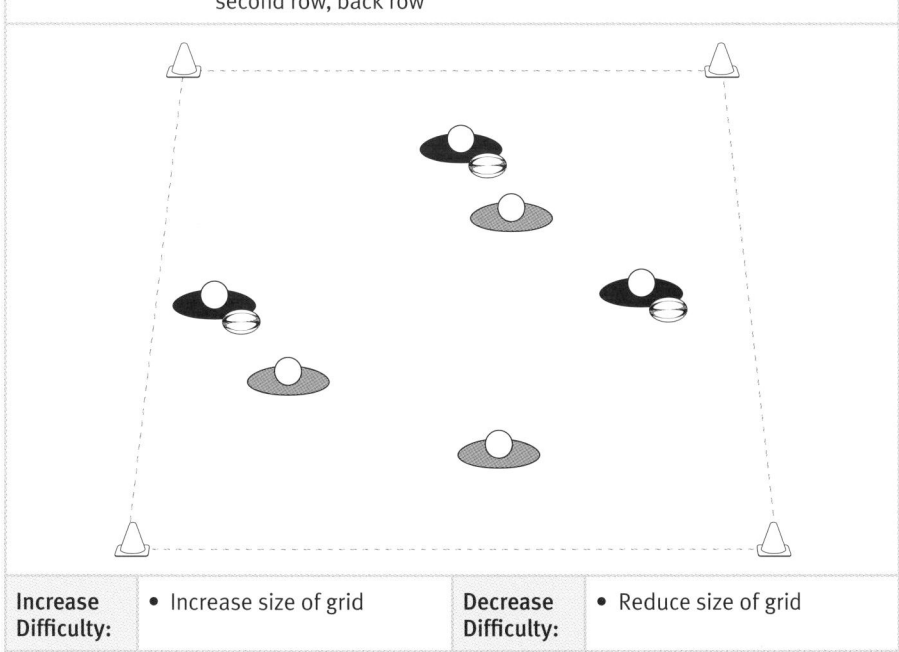

Relevant Positions: Back three, centre, fly-half, scrum-half, prop forward, hooker, second row, back row

Increase Difficulty:	• Increase size of grid	Decrease Difficulty:	• Reduce size of grid

Key Coaching Points / Questions:

Must be supervised by an appropriately qualified coach

Basic tackle technique key points
- Cheek to cheek (face cheek to bottom cheek)
- Ring of steel with arms around opponent
- Drive through the target
- Get to feet quickly

Offensive tackle technique key points
- Look up through the tackle
- Move same side foot forwards to shoulder making contact
- Get feet as close to opponent as possible
- Hit up through the tackle
- Shoulder above hips
- Grab one leg of the ball carrier and lift
- Land on top of ball carrier and pin his back to the ground
- If no longer on feet, keep the opponent pinned to the ground, plant feet and rip ball, or seal the ball in, if player is not releasing

Progression 1:
Players start on knees, with no hand-offs/fends.

Progression 2:
Walking only, with no hand-offs/fends.

Progression 3:
Running, with no hand-offs/fends.

Progression 4:
Hand-offs/fends allowed in the practice.

PRACTICE 27

Title: Repetitive tackle drill	**Time:** 10 minutes
	Kit: Balls, cones

Objective: Develop player's ability to react to runners from different directions and force them to the floor	**Organisation:** Groups of 4
Game Principles: Go forwards	**Grid Size:** Triangle with 15m sides

Description:
- Player to stand in the centre of the triangle surrounded by a ball carrier at each corner
- Ball carriers to run one at a time across the triangle to the opposite side in an attempt to score a try
- Ball carrier must stay inside the triangle at all times
- Player to bring ball carrier to the floor before he gets to the opposite side of the triangle
- Upon completion of the tackle or the scoring of the try, player is to get to his feet, return to the middle of the triangle and make a tackle on the next runner

Relevant Positions: Back three, centre, fly-half, scrum-half, prop forward, hooker, second row, back row

Increase Difficulty:	• Player to start on one knee • Full pace	**Decrease Difficulty:**	• Walking pace

Key Coaching Points / Questions:

Must be supervised by an appropriately qualified coach

- Stay in a low position and light on toes
- Small steps to cover the ground quickly
- Head to the side of the ball carrier (cheek to cheek)
- Chin off chest
- Arms wide to attract runner
- Initial contact with shoulder on the thighs of the ball carrier
- Wrap arms tight around legs of the ball carrier
- Use legs to drive ball carrier to the ground
- Push off the ball carrier on the ground and get to feet quickly
- Use either shoulder

Progression:

Reduce time between tackles.

Extend the time per activity: begin with six tackles per rotation, then aim to complete twelve without a rest.

SCRUM

Practice games in this section:

28. The power crawl and tyre push

29. Body shape in the scrum

30. Body management in the scrum

31. Scrum

32. Scrummaging in units

PRACTICE 28

Title: The power crawl and tyre push	Time: 10 minutes
	Kit: Tyres
Objective: Practise correct body position and shape	Organisation: Second-row units
Game Principles: Regain possession at scrum	Grid Size: 10m channel
Description: • Player adopts correct body position on all fours • Player to crawl forwards powerfully and slowly while maintaining a good body position throughout	
Relevant Positions: Prop forward, hooker, second row, back row	

Increase Difficulty:	• Add resistance to the crawl using tackle shield	Decrease Difficulty:	• N/A

Key Coaching Points / Questions:

Maintain correct and safe body position:

- Head in a neutral position
- Shoulders pulled back
- Chest out and engage the core
- Flat back
- Keep hips below shoulders
- Bend at waist and flex the knees
- Feet shoulder width apart and working on balls of feet (avoid splaying the feet)

Progression 1:

Once technique is perfected, have two opposing players crawl towards each other. When they meet, go through correct engagement sequence and have 1 v 1 driving competition.

Progression 2:

Player tries to drive the tyre forwards while maintaining good body shape.

SMALL-SIDED GAMES

PRACTICE 29

Title: Body shape in the scrum	Time: 10 minutes
	Kit: Balls, cones

Objective: Practise correct body position and shape.	Organisation: Individual practice.
Game Principles: Regain possession at scrum	Grid Size: 5m x 5m

Description:
- Player adopts correct body position against a suitably sized Swiss ball
- Ball provides a safe training aid against which to scrummage and improve technique
- Player should experiment with packing against both the left and right of the ball (see the second figure below)
- Initially the ball should be stabilised by a coach/player

Relevant Positions: Prop forward, hooker, second row, back row

Increase Difficulty:	• Move across Swiss ball and maintain shape • Destabilise Swiss ball	Decrease Difficulty:	• Remain stationary • Stabilise Swiss ball

Key Coaching Points / Questions:

Must be supervised by an appropriately qualified coach

Maintain correct and safe body position:

- Head in a neutral position
- Shoulders pulled back
- Chest out and engage the core
- Flat back
- Bend at waist and flex the knees
- Feet shoulder width apart and working on balls of feet (avoid splaying the feet)

Progression 1:
Player moves across the ball from left to right while maintaining correct technique. Ball is kept stabilised by a coach/player.

Progression 2:
As above, but the ball is now freestanding and unstable.

Progression 3:
Introduce an opposition player and make the practice competitive. Each player attempts to push the ball under his opposite number while maintaining correct technique and body position. It is important that correct shape is maintained throughout.

PRACTICE 30

Title: Body management in the scrum	**Time:** 10 minutes
	Kit: N/A
Objective: Practise correct body position and shape.	**Organisation:** Front-row, second-row, back-row units
Game Principles: Regain possession at scrum	**Grid Size:** 5m x 5m

Description:
- Two props work against each other to improve individual technique and body shape
- Practice begins in an uncontested manner and builds up to be fully contested
- At all times the practice must be fully controlled with the emphasis on safety, correct technique and maintaining good body shape
- To improve stability in the exercise it is good practice to have two players scrum against a single player

Relevant Positions: Prop forward, hooker, second row, back row

Increase Difficulty:	• Increase levels of contest • Increase time	**Decrease Difficulty:**	• Reduce levels of contest • Decrease time

Key Coaching Points / Questions:

Must be supervised by an appropriately qualified coach

Maintain correct and safe body position:

- Head in a neutral position
- Shoulders pulled back
- Chest out and engage the core
- Flat back
- Bend at waist and flex the knees
- Feet shoulder width apart and working on balls of feet (avoid splaying the feet)
- Reinforce correct engagement sequence of 'CROUCH, TOUCH, PAUSE, ENGAGE'

Progression 1:

Under control, the players lower and raise the height of the 1 v 1 scrum. It is important that they work cooperatively to maintain balance and good body shape.

Progression 2:

Under the same controlled conditions as above the players move left and right, forwards and backwards, and rotate in clockwise and counter-clockwise directions.

Progression 3:

Players engage in a controlled manner and, under the direction of the coach, attempt to drive the other player backwards in a straight line. At all times, they must maintain correct technique and good shape. The coach could introduce an element of competition with a scoring system, for instance 'best of five'.

PRACTICE 31

Title: Scrum	Time: 30 minutes (max)
	Kit: Scrum machine
Objective: Improve the ability of the hooker to scrummage as part of a unit.	Organisation: Front-row unit
Game Principles: Safety, body position, scrum engagement procedure	Grid Size: N/A
Description: *Note:* The scrum is a potentially dangerous place – *practice must always be supervised* • Once the correct body positions and shapes have been mastered the front-row, second-row and back-row units can be put together to practise scrummaging against a scrum machine or opposition. • Involve the scrum-half in this practice and at each stage in development, practise with the scrum-half feeding the ball to the scrum and the hooker directing the ball to the back of the scrum to restart the game.	
Relevant Positions: Prop forward, hooker, second row, back row, scrum-half	

Increase Difficulty:	• Start with unopposed against scrum machine • Progress to opposed scrummaging	Decrease Difficulty:	• Revert to individual coaching until techniques are mastered

Key Coaching Points / Questions:

Must be supervised by an appropriately qualified coach

Practices should include individual work, work with the props, and work with the scrum-half:

- Work on timing of the strike of the ball, speed of the strike, and direction
- Practise body position for the strike and for the eight-man shove
- After practising with the props, introduce locks and eventually the whole pack
- Remember to use the correct engagement sequence 'CROUCH, TOUCH, PAUSE, ENGAGE' every time the players go into a scrum position
- Make sure that the props take their timing from the hooker and that they are not rushing ahead and disrupting the timing
- Talk to the locks about not pushing before the engagement as this can force the hooker and the props into uncomfortable and dangerous positions

Progression 1:

Start with just the hooker to observe and correct the body position. Introduce the scrum-half to practise timing of the signal and strike.

Progression 2:

Introduce the two props and work on binds and body position. Again introduce the scrum-half to practise timing of the signal and strike.

Progression 3:

Introduce the two second-row players and finally build up to the full pack. Again repeat practice with the scrum-half.

PRACTICE 32

Title: Scrummaging in units	Time: 10 minutes
	Kit: Scrummage machine (if not enough players)
Objective: Introduce and develop the locks' bind with their prop (see figure below, players on the right) and with each other (see figure below, players on the left), while maintaining body position and shape	Organisation: Front-row, second-row units
Game Principles: Regain possession at scrum	Grid Size: 5m x 5m
Description: • Scrummaging units of prop, hooker and lock engage against each other in a 2 v 1 contest • Develop the scrum into a 3 v 3 and then up to a 5 v 5 contest • Initially the practice is uncontested with the emphasis being on correct body shape and binding	
Relevant Positions: Prop forward, hooker, second row, back row	

Increase Difficulty:	• Introduce movement • Introduce contest	Decrease Difficulty:	• Remain stationary

Key Coaching Points / Questions:

Must be supervised by an appropriately qualified coach

Maintain correct and safe body position:
- Head in a neutral position
- Shoulders pulled back
- Chest out and engage the core
- Flat back
- Bend at waist and flex the knees
- Feet shoulder width apart
- Second-row players' body position slightly below that of the front row, as illustrated by the players in the figure opposite, with the line of force going through the seat of the front row
- Second row binds with the front row with either the wrap-around bind (shown above) or with the through-the-legs bind
- Second-row players take a strong, full-on bind with each other

Progression 1:
Focus is on the bind between prop and second row as illustrated in the figure above with the players on the right. The players on the left will bind up with both second-row players either side of the prop for stability in this practice, to enable the opposing unit to engage and work against them.

Progression 2:
Same as above but the focus now being on the bind between the two second-row players with the hooker between them. In this way, players can be rotated as the driving pressure is increased, to put them into a more realistic situation.

LINE-OUT

Practice games in this section:

33. Line-out jumping: Shadowing the jumper

34. Line-out supporting: Introducing safe technique

35. Line-out supporting: Safe technique

36. Line-out

PRACTICE 33

Title: Line-out jumping: Shadowing the jumper	Time: 10 minutes
	Kit: 1 ball, cones
Objective: Regaining possession at line-out	Organisation: U15 and below: Lineout without lifting, vary number of players.
	U16 and above: See practices 34 and 35
Game Principles: Contest possession, apply pressure	Grid Size: 2 cones 5 m apart (vary depending on number of players)

Description:
- Working between the cones, arrange two lines of players varying from one to three players per line
- Nominate an attacking and a defensive line
- Attacking line work together to put a player into space to receive the ball thrown from the touchline
- Defensive team tries to shadow the movement and reduce the space for the attacking team
- Coach can introduce an element of competition, giving points to the side that is most successful as an attacking team

Relevant Positions: Prop forward, hooker, second row, back row

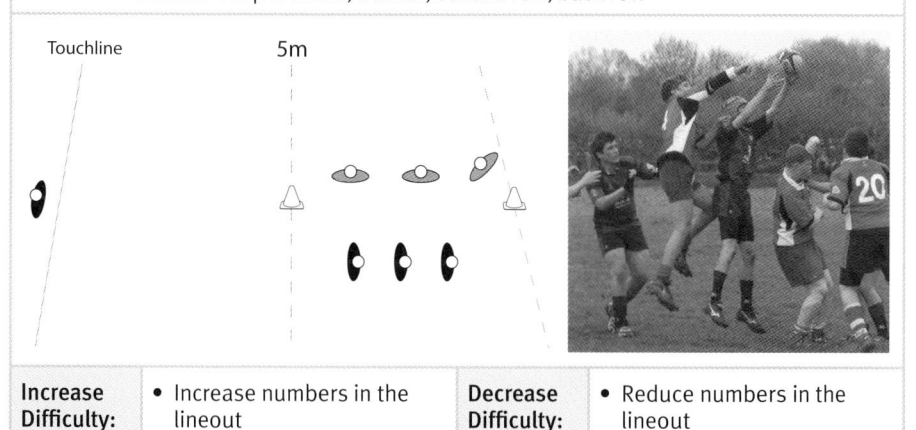

Increase Difficulty:	• Increase numbers in the lineout	Decrease Difficulty:	• Reduce numbers in the lineout

Key Coaching Points / Questions:

Must be supervised by an appropriately qualified coach

Attack team players

- Remain balanced at all times and move across the ground (lateral movement) under control
- Avoid getting too close to the other players, to allow freedom of movement
- Jump dynamically as if taking off from a springboard
- Keep elbows in and drive arms up high in front of head, keeping hands in a close catching position
- React to the jump and close on the jumper to form the line-out maul

Defending players

- Watch the feet of the attacking players
- React to the movement that 'triggers' the jump
- Cut down space for the attack

Progression:

Once the players are reacting effectively to the movement, coach may introduce the catch, maul and drive.

PRACTICE 34

Title: Line-out supporting: Introducing safe technique	**Time:** 10 minutes
	Kit: Contact shield, post protector tackle tube, Swiss ball
Objective: Introduce *safe* and effective lifting techniques	**Organisation:** Groups of 3 (1 jumper and 2 lifters)
Game Principles: Contest possession at line-out	**Grid Size:** 10m x 10m
Description: • Safe line-out supporting/lifting technique is practised • Facing each other, players should initially practise using a light training aid such as a contact shield or Swiss ball • The key factors should be continually reinforced throughout	
Relevant Positions: Prop forward, second row, back row	

SMALL-SIDED GAMES

| Increase Difficulty: | • Introduce lift | Decrease Difficulty: | • Remove lift |

Key Coaching Points / Questions:

Must be supervised by an appropriately qualified coach

- Strong and balanced body position – similar to that adopted for many lifts in the gym
- Support ball from underside with fingers-splayed grip as shown
- Work from low in the lift, keeping back straight and head in a neutral position
- Drive upwards with the legs and move inwards, to ensure maximum height and stability, finishing on tiptoe where possible
- The arms must be fully extended and locked out to ensure stability
- Introduce second lifter: lifters face each other and, using the same technique as described above, work together to develop combined lift

Progression 1:

Replace the contact shield with a post protector. The technique remains the same but the lifters will find the shape and weight of the post protector more difficult. The coach should use this time to identify and correct any weakness in the technique. Once the players have mastered the technique facing towards the 'player', the coach may wish to position them at right angles to the 'player' so they are facing the direction they would be playing in a game. This introduces a further element of movement. Again watch for correct and safe technique, and correct where necessary.

Progression 2:

As above but replace the post protector with a Swiss ball. The coach holds the ball between the two lifters and triggers the practice by calling 'Set!', at which point the coach bounces the ball between the lifters. The bounce imitates the movement of the jumper. The lifters must react to the call and movement and lift effectively. The Swiss ball is light and unstable and will highlight any imbalance or poor technique, especially in hand position.

Progression 3:

As above but replace with a tackle tube. The practice is very similar to progression 1 but the object being lifted is much heavier and more awkward. Once players are competent and safe at lifting in this controlled manner, lifting a player should be introduced.

PRACTICE 35

Title: Line-out supporting: Safe technique	Time: 10 minutes
	Kit: Balls, cones
Objective: Practise *safe* and effective lifting techniques	Organisation: Groups of 3 (1 jumper and 2 lifters)
Game Principles: Contest possession at line-out	Grid Size: 10m x 10m
Description: • Working between two cones set 5m apart, arrange two lines of 'pods' of three players per line • Nominate an attacking and a defensive line • Attacking line work together to get into space and support the jumper, who receives a ball thrown from the touchline • Defensive team tries to shadow the movement and reduce the space for the attacking team • Coach can introduce an element of competition, giving points to the side that is most successful as attacking team	
Relevant Positions: Prop forward, second row, back row	

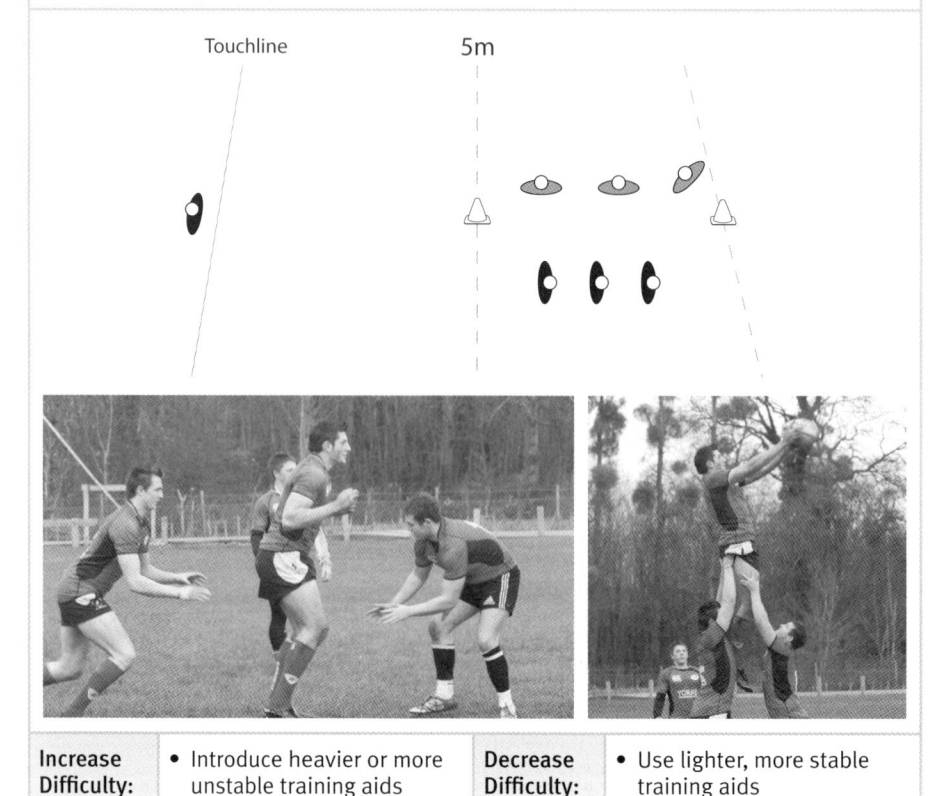

Increase Difficulty:	• Introduce heavier or more unstable training aids	Decrease Difficulty:	• Use lighter, more stable training aids

Key Coaching Points / Questions:

Must be supervised by an appropriately qualified coach

- Strong and balanced body position – similar to that adopted for many lifts in the gym
- Work from low in the lift, keeping back straight and head in a neutral position
- Avoid pre-gripping of the jumper – it is restrictive to his movement, signals your intentions to the opposition and may be unsafe
- Support jumper with palms facing upwards
- Rear supporter to place hands on the rear of the jumper's shorts, providing support below the buttocks
- Front supporter to place hands on the jumper's thighs – this may be below the shorts but must be above the knees
- Drive upwards with the legs and move inwards to ensure maximum height and stability, finishing on tiptoe where possible
- The arms must be fully extended and locked out to ensure stability
- The jumper must be returned to the ground safely under control

PRACTICE 36

Title: Line-out	**Time:** 30 minutes
	Kit: Swiss ball, target for hooker to practise throwing at
Objective: Practise accurate throwing	**Organisation:** Full pack
Game Principles: Safety and body position	**Grid Size:** Vary distance of throw

Description:
- Practise accurate throwing (e.g. throw to a target such as a rugby post, a mark on a wall or a player)
- Practise throwing the ball over the posts to gain timing and use whole-body action

Relevant Positions: Hooker

| Increase Difficulty: | • Reduce the width of the grid | Decrease Difficulty: | • Make the grid wider
• Condition defender to defend in predetermined channels or against certain attackers |

Key Coaching Points / Questions:

- Ball is held in a two-handed grip – practise with grip to find the most comfortable one
- Feet, hips and shoulders parallel to the touchline
- With knees slightly bent, arch back to bring stomach muscles into use during the throw
- Set up so that arms, hands and ball travel in a straight line in the direction of the centre of the line-out – this may mean keeping elbows in close to the head
- Throw and at the same time pull through the stomach muscles to give power to the throw
- Follow through, keeping hands and arms pointing at the ball, and drive body high onto the toes
- Don't always work with the same type of ball – try to vary conditions, e.g. wet ball, slippery ball and different makes of ball
- Practise the most difficult throws at least as much as the easier throws!
- Practise throwing at a target while a friend attempts to distract or talk to the player

Progression 1:
Start with hooker working on technique by throwing at a target.

Progression 2:
Develop single jumping 'pods' to work on timing and flight / delivery of the ball.

Progression 3:
Progress to full line-out and practise full range of throws in simulated game situation.

CHAPTER 10
GAMES FOR UNDERSTANDING

These are games for larger numbers of participants and are designed to highlight specific tactical elements in the game, such as defensive patterns or exploiting back-line space. In these games players are put into game-related situations, and coaches should encourage their players to experiment and explore alternative ways of gaining advantage from each situation. Generally, there is no right or wrong way to play these games but, coached in this way, players develop their own tactics and routines, which are easily transferred from the training ground to match day.

Coaches should encourage players to relate their actions and tactics to the 'principles of play' as discussed below. This will not only help players to understand their decisions but will also provide a general framework for playing in the broader game. Games for understanding need more structure and organisation and should be planned and delivered under the direction of a qualified coach.

Practice games in this chapter:

37. Jailbreak

38. Outside channel: Wide passing

39. 4 v 2

40. Line-out end ball

41. Fijian touch

42. Numbers touch

43. Parramatta touch

44. Five lives

45. Ruck and maul

46. Organising back-line defence

47. Operating a drift defence

48. Counter-attack

49. Defensive line game

50. Attacking a drift defence

PRACTICE 37

Title: Jailbreak *(Can also be used as a good contact warm-up game)*	Time: 10 minutes
	Kit: Balls, bibs, cones
Objective: Improve ability to cover gaps and close down players trying to break through defensive gaps, and tackle effectively	Organisation: Groups of 6–10
Game Principles: Defend and apply pressure	Grid Size: 15m x 15m

Description: *If played as a contest game, must be supervised by an appropriately qualified coach*

- Ball carriers move around in safe area
- Defenders are not allowed in safe area
- Coach shouts 'Jailbreak!'
- Attackers are now allowed out of the safe area and defenders are allowed in
- Attackers try to reach the outside limit of the 15m grid
- Defenders stop attackers by tackling
- Once attackers reach the outer limit, or all are tackled, then play stops
- Each tackle made = 1 point for defender, each try scored = 1 point for attack
- Roles are reversed and scores are recorded
- When used as a warm-up, develop from touch tackle to holding tackle to wrestle

Relevant Positions: Back three, centre, fly-half, scrum-half, prop forward, hooker, second row, back row

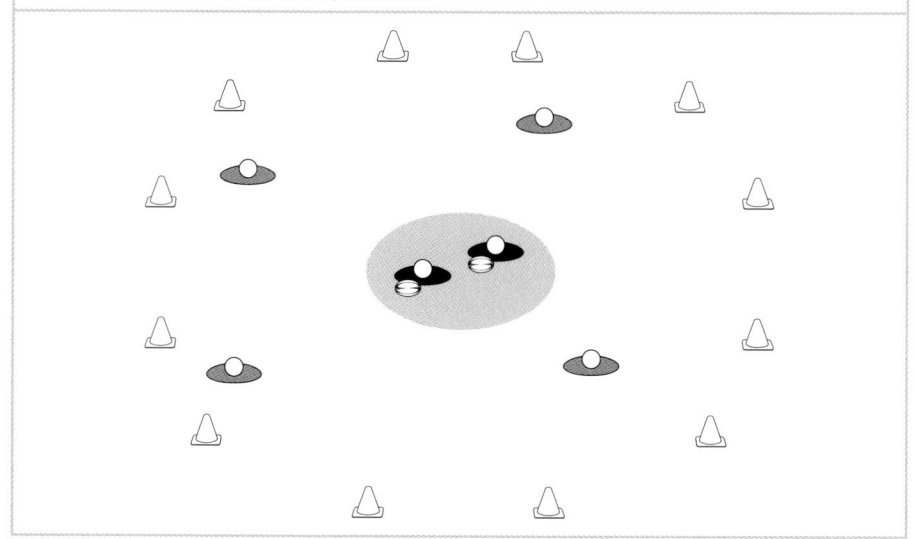

Increase Difficulty:	• Running allowed • Ball must be stripped from attacker	Decrease Difficulty:	• All players move on knees • Players walking

Key Coaching Points / Questions:

Basic tackle technique key points

- Cheek to cheek (face cheek to bottom cheek)
- Ring of steel with arms around opponent
- Drive through the target
- Get to feet quickly

Offensive tackle technique key points

- Look up through the tackle
- Move same side foot forwards to shoulder making contact
- Get feet as close to opponent as possible
- Hit up through the tackle
- Grab one leg of the ball carrier and lift
- Land on top of ball carrier and pin his back to the ground
- If no longer on feet, keep opponent pinned to the floor, plant feet and rip ball, or seal the ball in, if player is not releasing

Progression 1:

All players move on knees.

Progression 2:

On feet, only walking allowed.

Progression 3:

Running allowed.

Progression 4:

Ball must be stripped from attacker within the laws of rugby.

PRACTICE 38

Title: Outside channel: Wide passing

Time: 10 minutes

Kit: Balls, bibs, cones

Objective: Improve the ability to use a long-range pass to supply ball to outside players in space.

Organisation: Two teams of 3–4 players in each team

Game Principles: Give and take passes

Grid Size: 15m x 30m

Description:
- Ball starts on attackers' try line
- One player from the attacking team must stay in each of the outside channels
- Once a touch is made, defenders must retire onside and touched player places ball and uses scrum-half pass to restart game
- Teams rotate roles once a try is scored or 2 minutes is up, whichever is sooner
- Knock-on results in play restarting from try line

Relevant Positions: Back three, centre, fly-half, scrum-half

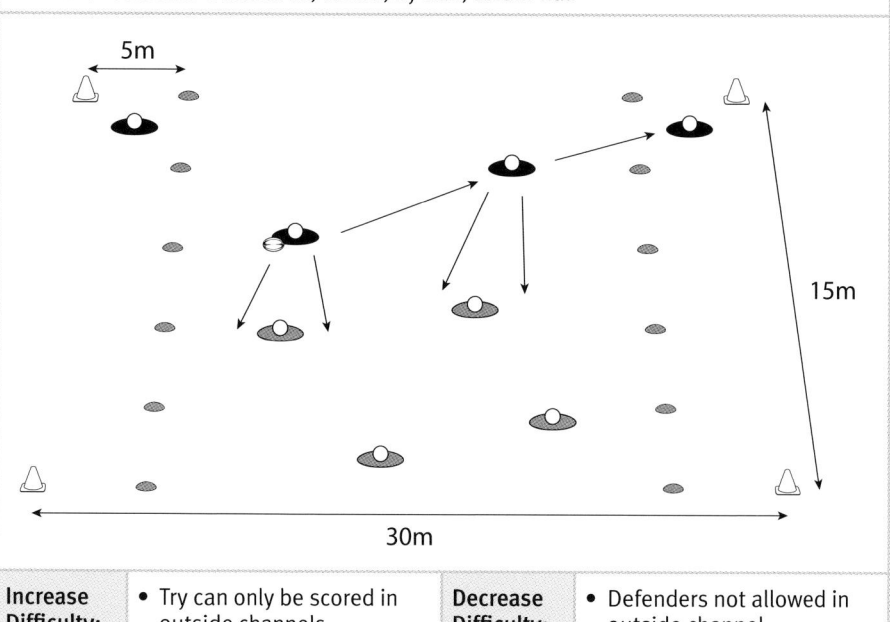

Increase Difficulty:	• Try can only be scored in outside channels • Widen the grids	Decrease Difficulty:	• Defenders not allowed in outside channel • Bring post players close together

Key Coaching Points / Questions:

Game key points
- Fix defenders in centre field to create space in side channels
- Play ball flat on gain line
- Attack at pace to hold the defenders

Defence
- Close down attackers space
- Identify ball carrier and, when ball is passed out, drift out
- Use sidelines as extra defenders
- Work as a unit – communicate defensive responsibility
- Player marking ball carrier stands slightly in front of other defenders

Miss pass key points (cut-out pass)
- Dummy runner angles line in towards passer to create more space for receiver
- Pass flat on the gain line
- Receiver hits the ball at pace
- Passer dummy passes to short runner

Spiral pass key points
- Turn the ball lengthways with fingers across the seam
- Use the back hand to give power
- Use front hand to guide ball and add stability
- Follow through with hands finishing at target

Progression 1:
Try can only be scored in outside channels.

Progression 2:
Defenders are not allowed into the outside channel – they must use rush defence.

Progression 3:
Widen the grid to make passing to the outside channel in one pass harder.

PRACTICE 39

Title: 4 v 2	Time: 2 minutes then rotate players
	Kit: Balls, bibs, cones

Objective: Develop the ability to create and maintain space when an overlap occurs	Organisation: Groups of 6–10
Game Principles: Keep possession and apply pressure	Grid Size: 20m x 20m

Description:
- Group of four attackers start on cone A
- Group of two defenders start on cone C
- Play starts when attacking group starts to move
- Attackers run round cone B and attack opposite try line (between D and E)
- Defenders run around cone D and defend their try line
- Play stops when a try is scored, touch is made or knock-on occurs
- Play restarts from cones A and C

Relevant Positions: Back three, centre, fly-half, scrum-half

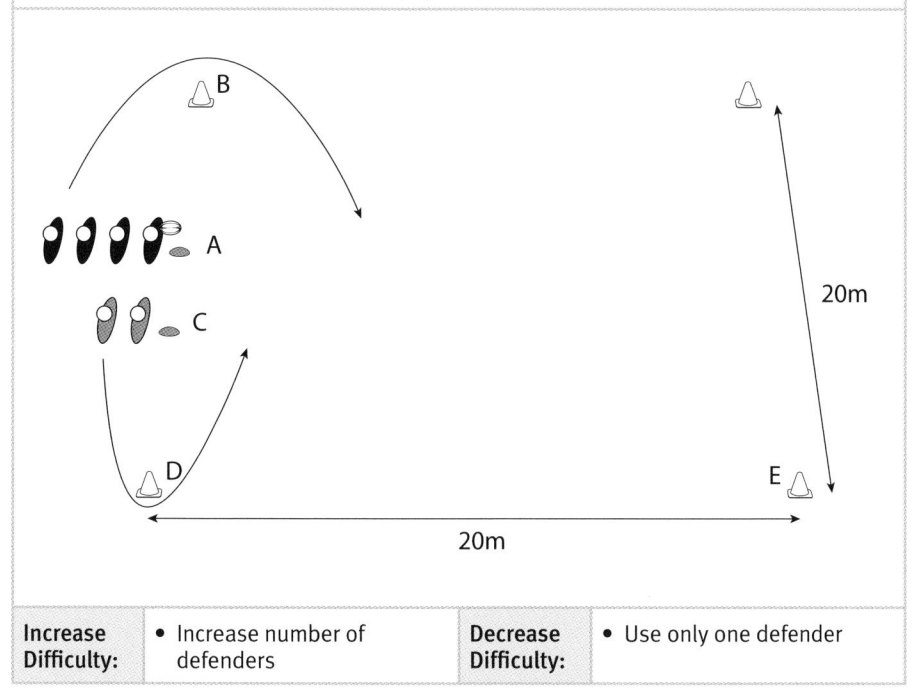

Increase Difficulty:	• Increase number of defenders	Decrease Difficulty:	• Use only one defender

Key Coaching Points / Questions:

Attack
- Attack inside shoulder of defender
- Run at pace
- Play the ball flat on the gain line
- If defenders turn hips outwards, attack inside

Defence
- Close down attackers' space
- Defenders set up opposite the inside shoulder of the attacker and when ball is passed out, drift out
- Use sidelines as extra defenders
- Work as a unit – communicate defensive responsibility
- Player marking ball carrier stands slightly in front of other defenders

Progression 1:
One defender starts from cone D, the other from cone E.

Progression 2:
Vary start position of attackers.

PRACTICE 40

Title: Line-out end ball	**Time:** 20 minutes
	Kit: Balls, bibs, cones
Objective: Develop ability of jumping pods to move together into space, jump and secure a thrown ball	**Organisation:** 8–20 line-out players and hookers
Game Principles: Line-out	**Grid Size:** 30m x 15m

Description:
- Pods of two support players and one jumper work as units in a grid, with a thrower at each end of the grid
- If the red thrower has the ball, the red pods are in attack and vice versa for the blue team
- Aim of the game is to score by catching the ball over the opponent's line
- Pods are free to move anywhere in the grid
- If the ball is successfully caught, i.e. red throw–red catch or blue throw–blue catch, the ball is placed on the floor at the point of catch and the thrower advances to the ball until a try is scored
- If the ball is intercepted or lost, the ball is turned over to the other side

Relevant Positions: Prop forward, hooker, second row, back row

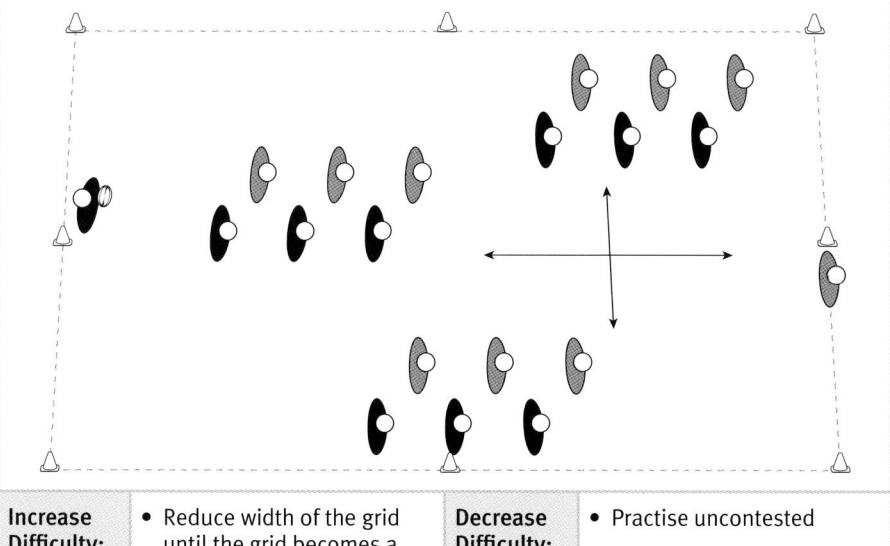

| Increase Difficulty: | • Reduce width of the grid until the grid becomes a line-out | Decrease Difficulty: | • Practise uncontested |

Key Coaching Points / Questions:

Must be supervised by an appropriately qualified coach

- Move together as a unit – communication is vital to effective movement
- Strong and balanced body position – similar to that adopted for many lifts in the gym
- Work from low in the lift, keeping back straight and head in a neutral position
- Avoid pre-gripping of the jumper – it is restrictive to his movement, signals your intentions to the opposition and may be unsafe
- Support jumper with palms facing upwards
- Rear supporter to place hands on the rear of the jumper's shorts, providing support below the buttocks
- Front supporter to place hands on the jumper's thighs – this may be below the shorts but must be above the knees
- Drive upwards with the legs and move inwards to ensure maximum height and stability, finishing on tiptoe where possible
- The arms must be fully extended and locked out to ensure stability
- The jumper must be returned to ground safely and under control

Progression:

Add more pods of support and jumpers to the practice.

PRACTICE 41

Title: Fijian touch	Time: 20 minutes
	Kit: Balls, cones
Objective: Improve spatial awareness, passing, communication, decision-making and evasion.	Organisation: Groups of 10–14
Game Principles: Go forwards into space and retain possession	Grid Size: 30m x 30m

Description:
- Normal rules of touch rugby apply except it takes two touches by two different defenders to make a tackle
- Play offload, through the legs or fast ruck touch

Relevant Positions: Back three, centre, fly-half, scrum-half, prop forward, hooker, second row, back row

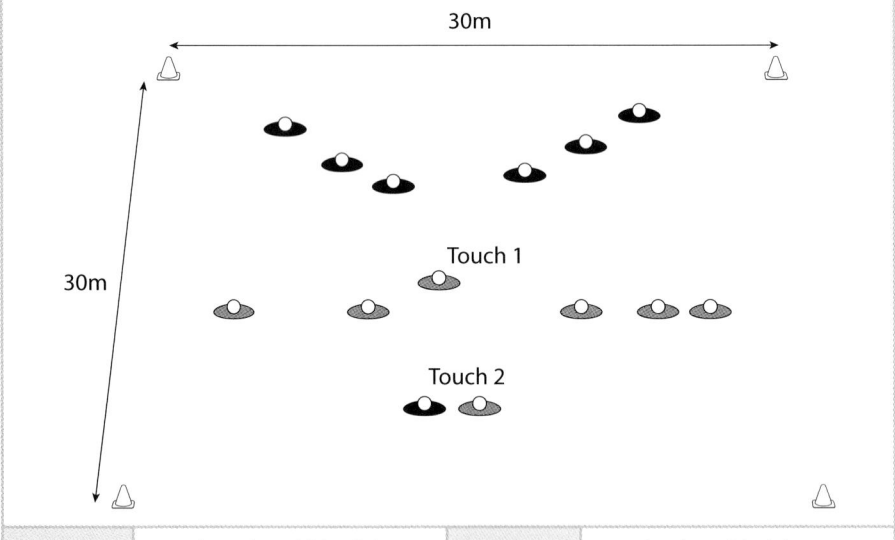

30m × 30m grid diagram showing Touch 1 and Touch 2 positions with cones

Increase Difficulty:	• Reduce the width of the grid • Introduce an extra defender at one or both ends	Decrease Difficulty:	• Make the grid wider • Reduce the number of defenders

Key Coaching Points / Questions:
- Importance of getting behind the defence
- Highlighting and beating a man one on one
- Attacking a cover defence

Progression 1:
After two touches, the game is restarted with a simple pass-off.

Progression 2:

After two touches, the game is restarted by throwing the ball in the air from between legs. Players close to the tackled player must react and get in support.

Progression 3:

After two touches, the game is restarted by setting up a fast ruck.

PRACTICE 42

Title: Numbers touch	**Time:** 20 minutes
	Kit: Balls, cones
Objective: Improve spatial awareness, use of space, communication, decision-making and evasion	**Organisation:** Groups of 10–14
Game Principles: Go forwards into space and retain possession	**Grid Size:** 30m x 30m

Description:
- Give equal numbers of players on both teams a number, either 1 or 2
- Normal rules of touch rugby apply
- When coach calls out either number 1 or number 2, the players on the defensive team with that number have to go down on one knee (out of the game)
- Players on the attacking team look for the spaces produced, communicate and attack those spaces
- Defence have to realign to cover for the lack of numbers
- Players are back in the game if there is a breakdown or try

Relevant Positions: Back three, centre, fly-half, scrum-half, prop forward, hooker, second row, back row

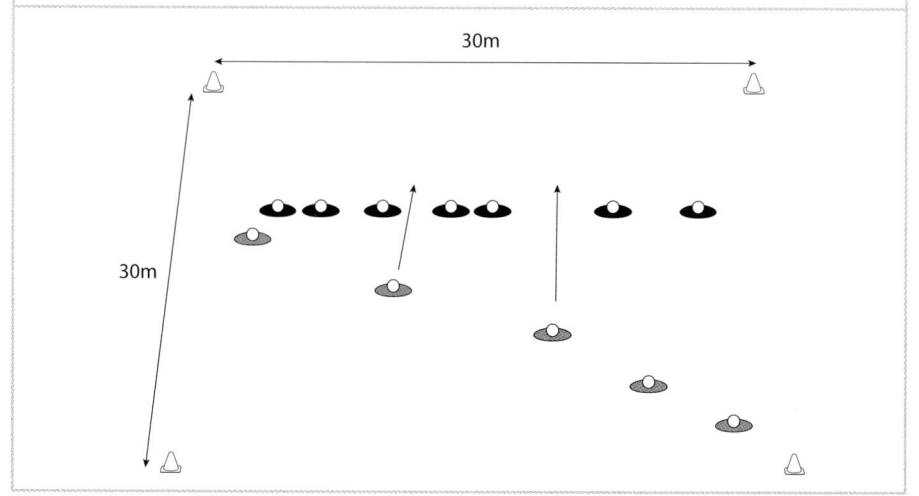

Increase Difficulty:	• Reduce the width of the grid • Introduce an extra defender at one or both ends	Decrease Difficulty:	• Make the grid wider • Reduce the number of defenders

Key Coaching Points / Questions:
- Importance of looking for space and communication
- Attack the space
- Defence must be aware of call, and cover for reduced numbers

Progression:
Rather than take defenders out on numbers, if a defender makes a touch tackle, he must retreat to his goal line before continuing in the game. This way only one defender is taken out at a time. May encourage defence to use a fullback to cover the space created when defenders are out of the game.

PRACTICE 43

Title: Parramatta touch	Time: 20 minutes
	Kit: 2 balls, cones
Objective: Improve spatial awareness, communication, decision-making and attacking into space	Organisation: Groups of 10–14
Game Principles: Attack weak defences – 3 v 2 v 1s	Grid Size: 60m x 40m

Description:
- Attack start from the centre cones and attack one defensive zone
- Attack only get one chance to score
- If this occurs, or there is a touch, dropped ball, forward pass etc., the attack turn around and immediately attack the far zone
- This continues for a set time dictated by the coaches
- If the attack score, the defence must run round the centre cones and get back to their defensive zone before the attack start attacking them again
- If defence make a touch they get a rest
- The defenders cannot defend outside of their zones

Relevant Positions: Back three, centre, fly-half, scrum-half

GAMES FOR UNDERSTANDING

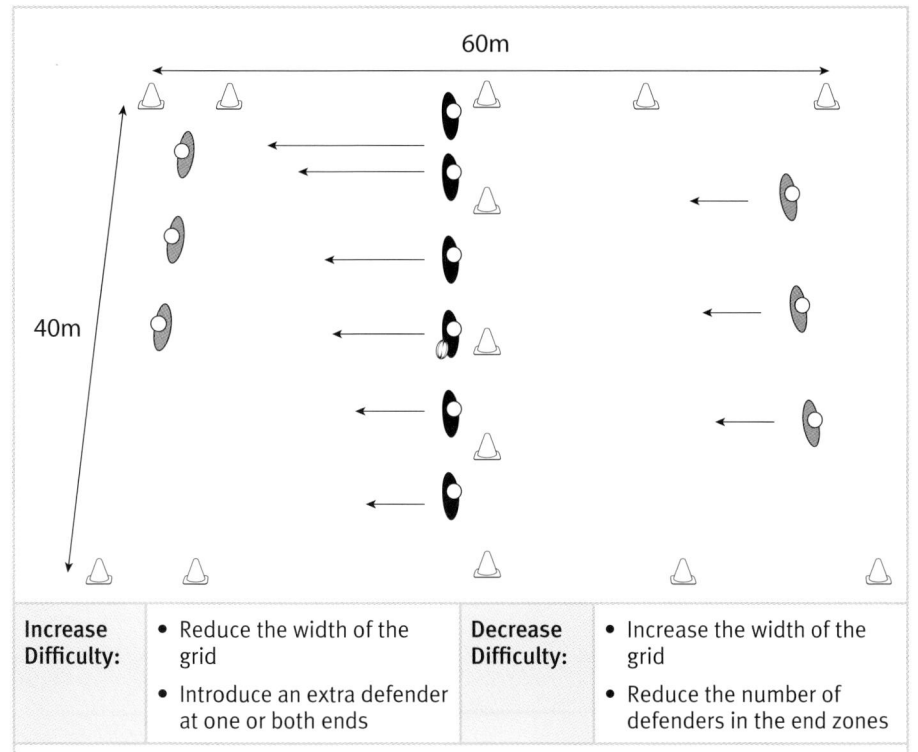

Increase Difficulty:	• Reduce the width of the grid • Introduce an extra defender at one or both ends	Decrease Difficulty:	• Increase the width of the grid • Reduce the number of defenders in the end zones

Key Coaching Points / Questions:

- Lines of running must be effective in order to score
- Attacking a drift defence and a blitz defence
- Realignment is essential in order to be effective continuously

Progression 1:
Coach may start the exercise with the players moving at a fast walking pace to accentuate the key factors of depth of the trailing players and the importance of moving the defenders to create space.

Progression 2:
Introduce extra defenders at one or both ends to put additional pressure on the attack.

Progression 3:
Reduce the width of the grid and remove players to create a 4 v 2, 3 v 2 and 2 v 1, to simulate attacks in a narrow blind-side channel, for example from a scrum near the touchline.

Progression 4:
Defenders must start in the defensive area but may move forwards out of the area once the attacking play has crossed the halfway line.

PRACTICE 44

Title: Five lives	Time: 10 minutes
	Kit: Ball, cones
Objective: Improve ability of players to attack and defend from first phase	Organisation: Groups of 15+
Game Principles: Go forwards, support, pressure, possession and communication	Grid Size: Half pitch

Description: From scrum or line-out:
- Five attempts are allowed to score (or defend the score)
- Scoring can be breaking the defensive line or actually scoring a try
- Back row positioned to support or defend as appropriate
- Game can be conditioned, having back row on knees or lying on stomachs

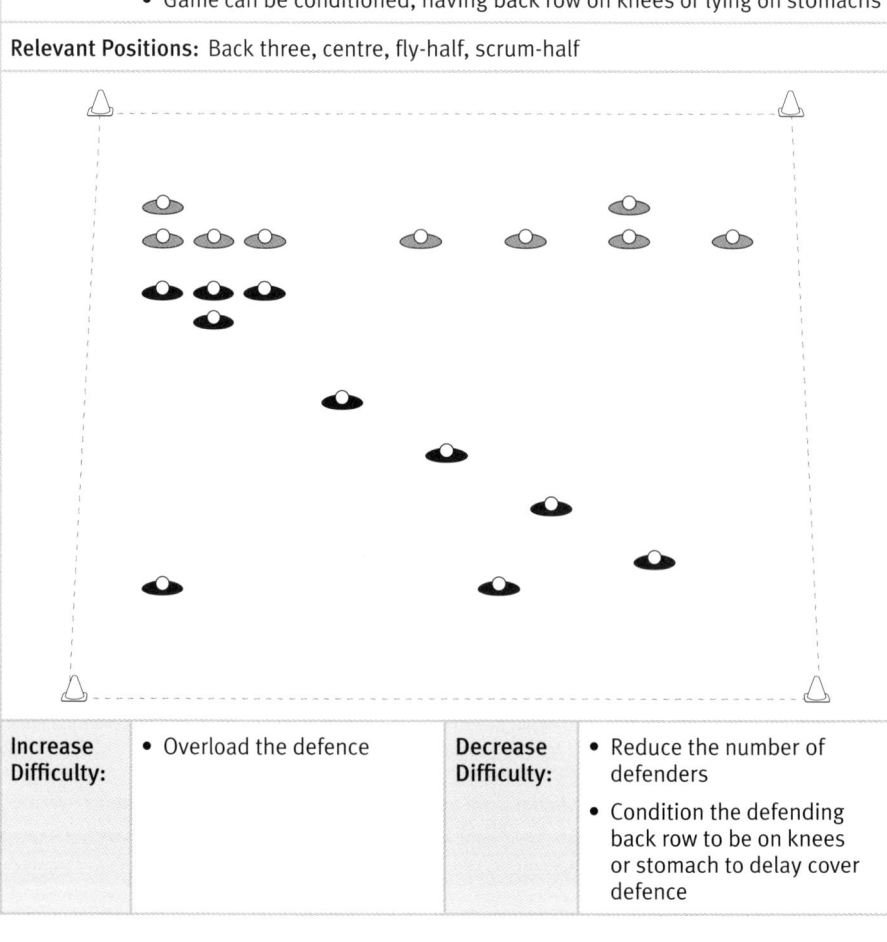

Relevant Positions: Back three, centre, fly-half, scrum-half

Increase Difficulty:	• Overload the defence	Decrease Difficulty:	• Reduce the number of defenders
			• Condition the defending back row to be on knees or stomach to delay cover defence

Key Coaching Points / Questions:

Attackers

- Continuous communication
- Read the game and look for space/gaps in defence
- Be first to support
- Commit defenders to create space elsewhere
- Run from depth and at angle to hold defenders
- Change setup to move defenders into weaker areas
- Stay strong in contact and look for offload

Defenders

- Continuous communication
- Apply pressure to the attack
- Drift/shepherd attackers in areas of strong defence
- Use touchline as extra defenders
- Strong in the tackle and compete for 50/50 ball

Progression 1:

Start with reduced numbers of defenders, or condition defending back row to start on knees or stomach.

Progression 2:

As attack become more successful put in additional defenders and remove any conditioning.

PRACTICE 45

Title: Ruck and maul	Time: 30 minutes
	Kit: Balls, tackle suits, cones
Objective: Improve players' ability to attack and defend in contact	Organisation: Groups of 11–14
Game Principles: Apply pressure, support, compete for possession, and decision-making	Grid Size: 20m x 20m

Description:
- When a player is held by only one defender, support player must rip the ball from his grasp and roll, pop or drive
- Developments to include decreasing size of pitch and allowing more defenders/support players in to build maul
- Eventually working in a very narrow channel – 5m – and working on the technique of building a driving maul
- Then back into the full-pitch game to use new techniques in a match context
- If defensive player can prevent release (he cannot turn attacker, only hold), the ball changes sides

Relevant Positions: Prop forward, hooker, second row, back row

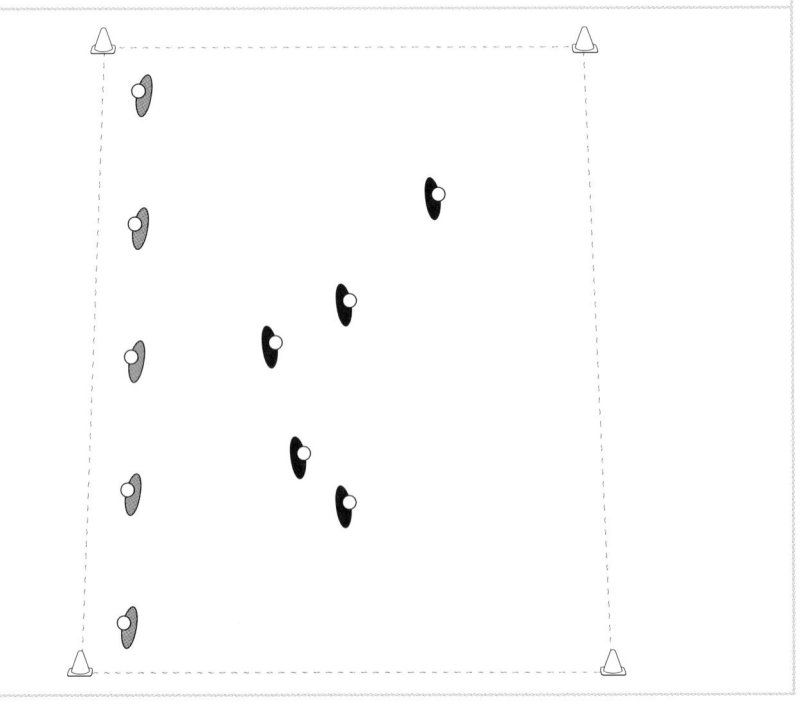

Increase Difficulty:	• Reduce the width of the grid • Aim to finish with 5m channel	Decrease Difficulty:	• Increase the width of the grid • Condition defenders to defend one at a time

Key Coaching Points / Questions:

Attackers

- Establish role of first and second support players
- Decide on when to ruck and when to maul
- Present ball away from opposition – low driving position from low to high
- Stay straight
- Secure ball by ripping downwards using strong shoulder muscles to free ball
- Ensure ball is secure
- Support new ball carrier either side and squeeze him backwards, rather than passing the ball, ensuring the ball carrier does not detach from the maul

Progression 1:

Start with only one defender allowed in contact and work on technique in the maul.

Progression 2:

Increase number of defenders allowed in contact. Reduce the width of the grid to condense both attack and defence.

PRACTICE 46

Title: Organising back-line defence	**Time:** 20–30 minutes
	Kit: 2–3 balls, cones, 5 channels
Objective: Develop organisation skills of players in defence	**Organisation:** Groups of 10–15
Game Principles: Go forwards, support and pressure	**Grid Size:** 40m x 50m

Description:
- Organise the practice as shown below using five channels
- Defenders line up opposite their attacker and within their channel, 20m away as if defending from a line-out
- Scrum-half plays the ball to the attacking fly-half who launches an attack
- Defending fly-half organises defence to press and apply pressure to the opposition
- 'Touch' tackle defence to begin
- Defence objective is to prevent the attack from scoring

Relevant Positions: Back three, centre, fly-half, scrum-half

THE RFU GUIDE TO COACHING POSITIONAL SKILLS

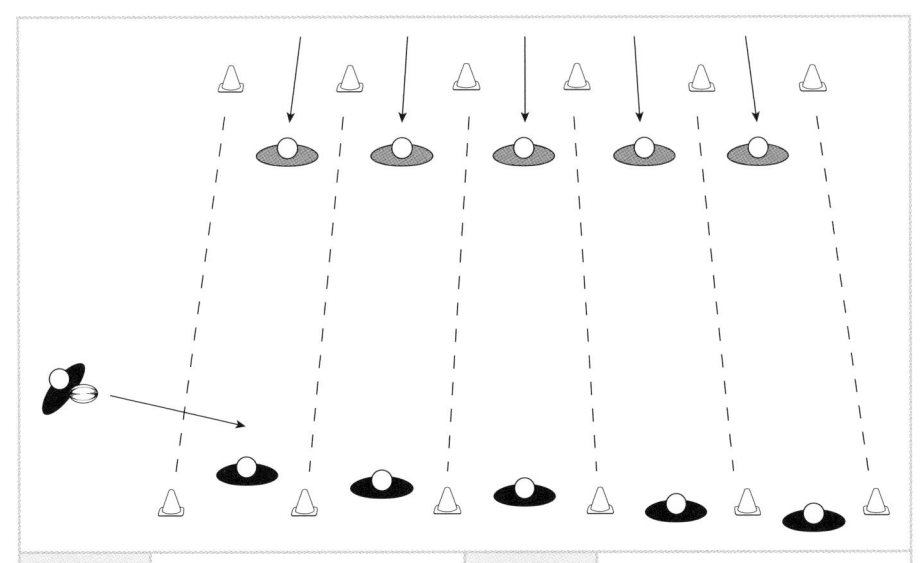

Increase Difficulty:	• Defenders to face away from opposition at start • Increase width of channels • Full contact	Decrease Difficulty:	• Begin at walking pace • Attackers not permitted to play a reverse ball inside

Key Coaching Points / Questions:

- Fly-half and support players to align themselves on inside shoulder of opposing attacker
- Fly-half to dictate the pace at which the line moves forwards – accelerate/decelerate
- Players to work with support either side to maintain alignment in defensive line
- Fly-half to promote communication across the defensive line
- Fly-half to look at moving forwards as quickly as possible
- Defence to cover ground quickly to start, slow down as they approach the tackle and accelerate into the tackle using small steps and getting feet close to the ball carrier

Progression 1:

Defence to be turned away from the attack and, on the call of the coach, turn and apply an organised defence.

Progression 2:

Organise the defence as if from a scrum situation, giving the opposition less space to attack.

Defenders may wish to experiment with different types of defence; drift (in to out defence), man on man, or out in defence.

PRACTICE 47

Title: Operating a drift defence	Time: 20–30 minutes
	Kit: 2–3 balls, cones, 5 channels
Objective: Defend pitch space when outnumbered in defence, and deny and prevent opposition from scoring	Organisation: Groups of 10–15
Game Principles: Go forwards, support and pressure	Grid Size: 40m x 50m

Description:
- Organise the practice as shown below using five channels
- First four defenders line up opposite first four attackers within designated channel, 10m away as if defending from a breakdown
- Scrum-half plays the ball to the attacking fly-half, who launches an attack
- Defending fly-half organises defence to press, drift and apply pressure to the opposition
- 'Touch' tackle defence to begin

Relevant Positions: Back three, centre, fly-half, scrum-half

Increase Difficulty:	• Defenders to face away from opposition at start	Decrease Difficulty:	• Begin at walking pace
	• Increase width of channels		• Attackers not permitted to play a reverse ball inside
	• Full contact		

Key Coaching Points / Questions:

- Fly-half and support players to align themselves on inside shoulder of opposing attacker
- Fly-half to dictate the pace at which the line moves forwards – accelerate/decelerate
- Defenders to remain just behind the running line of the inside defender as they press forwards
- Players to work with support either side to maintain defensive alignment
- As soon as the pass is made from fly-half to inside centre, defensive fly-half is to call a drift defence
- Defenders change their running line to that of the inside shoulder of next defender
- Defender to keep attacker in front of his hips
- Fly-half to control the line speed of the defence
- Defensive line looking to force the attack wide away from support and towards/into touch

Progression 1:
Defence to be turned away from the attack and, on the call of the coach, turn and apply an organised defence.

Progression 2:
Increase width of the channel so that the defence have to manage their position and pace in defence without being wrong-footed.

Progression 3:
Reduce to three defenders and develop the ability of the fly-half to apply pressure to ball carrier and immediate players to the outside by blocking off any reverse pass. Defenders must not press too quickly and find themselves outflanked by the attack. Defenders must be able to hold their depth and cover the ground quickly as they shuffle across the attacking line.

PRACTICE 48

Title: Counter-attack	Time: 30 minutes
	Kit: Balls, cones
Objective: Improve ability of back three to communicate and execute counter-attacking moves	Organisation: Groups of 10–15
Game Principles: Go forwards, support and pressure	Grid Size: Half pitch

Description:
- The back three line up to defend a tactical kick – diagram shows the kick taken from point 'B'
- One of the back three makes a decision on the best action to counter-attack and communicates this to other members of the back three
- In the case shown, No. 11 has caught the ball and passed infield to No. 15, No. 11 loops No. 15 to provide an attacking option midfield and No. 14 has realigned to provide support
- Chasing players No. 1, No. 2 and No. 3 can be introduced and conditioned to run at different angles to challenge the decision-making of the back three
- Progressions include taking kicks from 'A', 'B', 'C' or 'D' and testing the back three under the high ball, and cross-field and 'box' kicks
- When the situation has been played out, players return to their start positions and the exercise is repeated

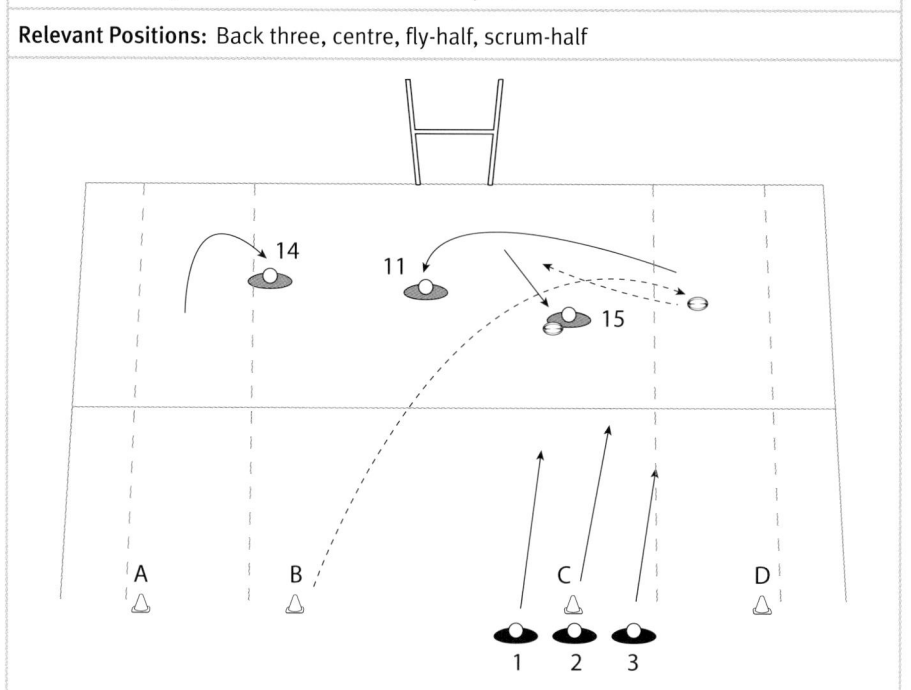

Relevant Positions: Back three, centre, fly-half, scrum-half

Increase Difficulty:	• Introduce players chasing the kick • Start chasing players from different points 'A', 'B', 'C' and 'D' • Vary the kick: high ball, long kick, grubber	Decrease Difficulty:	• Carry out the exercise without chasing players • Begin with just one ball

Key Coaching Points / Questions:

Back three

- Good clear and decisive call for the ball
- Communicate intentions to the others in the back three
- Ball carrier runs to fix chasing players and preserve space for the attack
- Others realign to provide attacking options and make use of available space for the attack
- Provide continuous support throughout the play

Chasing players

- Start from an onside position – coach may choose to delay chasing players while developing the exercise
- Communicate and keep a defensive line without dog-legs or gaps
- Communicate and run defensive patterns that limit attacking options and make best use of touchline and dead-ball areas touch

Progression 1:

Coach may start by sending chasing players out individually to allow space for the back three to work on counter-attack options.

Progression 2:

Move kicker and chasing players between cones 'A', 'B', 'C' and 'D'. Run the exercise with kicker and chasing players at different starting cones.

PRACTICE 49

Title: Defensive line game	**Time:** 2 minutes
	Kit: Balls, bibs, cones

Objective: Create space in a limited area to improve ability to achieve penetration	**Organisation:** Groups of 6
Game Principles: Run into space	**Grid Size:** 20m x 30m

Description:
- Attackers run round starting cone and attack opposition try line
- Defenders can start once the attackers pass the start cone
- Defenders are not allowed past their defensive limit
- If a touch is made, the ball must be passed back into the safe zone and play restarted
- If a try is scored, ball is passed to safe zone and play restarted
- After 2 minutes change defenders

Relevant Positions: Back three, centre, fly-half, scrum-half, prop forward, hooker, second row, back row

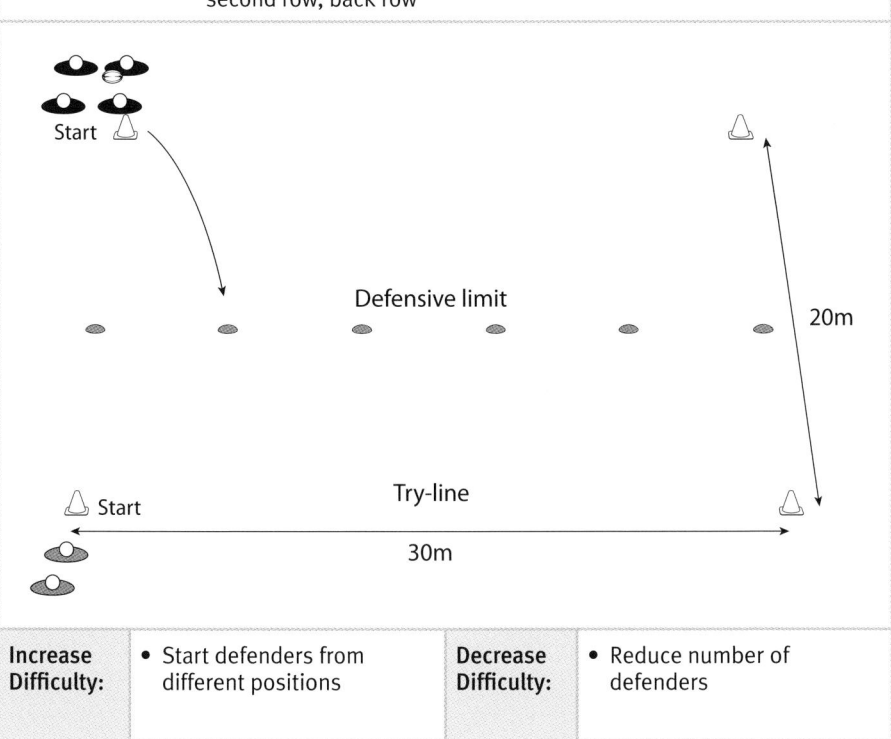

Increase Difficulty:	• Start defenders from different positions	**Decrease Difficulty:**	• Reduce number of defenders

Key Coaching Points / Questions:

Game key points

- Vary running lines to open space in defence
- Use switch pass and miss pass to create space
- Don't cross into defensive zone until space has opened up
- Play ball flat along gain line
- Run at pace to fix defenders
- Fix inside shoulder of defenders to create space on the outside

Pop pass key points

- Ball carrier turns to face towards receiving player
- Receiver raises hands giving target for the pass
- Ball is flicked into the air with the hands
- Receiver runs on to the ball at pace close to the passer

Miss pass key points

- Dummy runner angles line in towards passer to create more space for receiver
- Pass flat on the gain line
- Receiver hits the ball at pace
- Passer dummy passes to short runner

Switch pass

- Ball carrier runs at gap between two defenders
- Receiver runs towards outside space, then changes running line to cross behind ball carrier
- Ball is 'popped' into the air towards the receiving player

Progression:

Start defenders from different positions.

PRACTICE 50

Title: Attacking a drift defence	Time: 20 minutes
	Kit: Balls, bibs, cones
Objective: Improve spatial awareness, communication, decision-making and attacking into space	Organisation: Groups of 10–14
Game Principles: Attack a drift defence	Grid Size: 30m x 30m

Description:
- Normal touch rugby, but when a player from the attacking team is touched, all the players from the defending team must run in and touch the ball and drop to one knee
- Only when scrum-half plays the ball can the defence go, so forcing them to use a drift defence
- Attack have four phases to score until switch of roles

Relevant Positions: Back three, centre, fly-half, scrum-half, prop forward, hooker, second row, back row

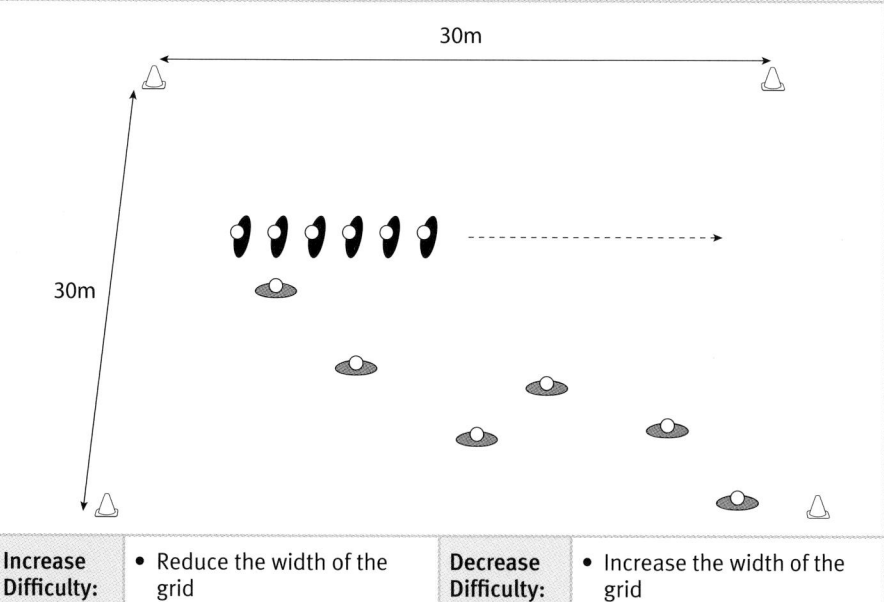

Increase Difficulty:	• Reduce the width of the grid • Introduce extra defenders	Decrease Difficulty:	• Increase the width of the grid • Reduce the number of defenders

Key Coaching Points / Questions:
- Adjust lines of running to 'fix' and hold defenders
- Use foot work and passes to put players into space
- Promote use of option and strike runners
- No pre-calls, so the attack react to what they see

Progression 1:

Coach may start the exercise with the players moving at a fast walking pace to accentuate the key factors of depth of the trailing players and the importance of 'fixing' defenders to create space.

Progression 2:

Introduce extra defenders to put additional pressure on the attack.

GLOSSARY

Blind side	The short space on the pitch between the breakdown or set piece and the touchline
Blitz defence	A line of defenders rushing up and putting pressure on the attack
Box kick	A kick over the shoulder (usually by the scrum-half) in situations where the ball is kicked from a static position (e.g. scrum, ruck or maul)
Breakdown	A break in the continuity of play, usually by a tackle, when the ball may be available for contest and turnover
Core muscles	Group of muscles, also known as the 'core', that work together to align the spine, ribs and pelvis
Counter-attack	A manoeuvre by the defending team after regaining the ball, whereby its defence is turned into an attack
Dog-leg	The defenders moving up out of alignment, leaving gaps in their defensive line
Drift defence	The defenders pushing the attackers towards the touchline and usually using the open-side flanker as an extra man as cover inside the defending fly-half
Defensive wall	A line of defenders, usually on the back foot of the hindmost player in rucks and mauls, or a defensive line that pushes up on the attackers following a kick ahead
Fixing a defender	When the ball carrier runs at a defender and commits him to the tackle before he releases the pass
Fringes	Generally the areas at the edges of, and close to, a ruck, maul or scrum
Gain line	The imaginary line that is parallel to the goal line and runs across the pitch at the point where there is a breakdown or set piece (e.g. ruck, maul, scrum or line-out)
Grubber kick	A kick where the ball travels end-over-end along the ground, usually used in attacking situations when it is aimed between two defenders
Lateral/backward pass	A ball that is passed so that it does not go forward of its point of release
Man to man	A defence tactic where each defender stands opposite, and takes, his respective attacking player

Mark	When a player calls 'Mark!' and catches the ball cleanly in his 22-metre area, he is allowed a free kick from the point where he caught the ball
Open side	The large space on the pitch between the breakdown or set piece and the touchline
Option runners	Attacking players who run as if they will receive the ball, but may continue their attacking line without it and therefore deceive the defence
Overlap/overload	Situation in which the attacking players outnumber the defending players, therefore providing an opportunity for some attacking players to be put into space with no defender to stop them
Pop pass	A pass over a short distance in a looping curve towards the receiver, using mainly the wrists to lift the ball into the air
Realign	When the defenders or attackers get back to their recognised positions in order to be more effective, usually after a phase of play has happened
Reverse pass	A pass made in the reverse direction to the way the passer is facing. The pass is delivered out of the back of the hands and generally behind the body.
Sidestep	A rapid change of a player's direction of run to beat a defender
Spin pass	A pass over a long distance in a flat line towards the receiver, using the wrists and arms to rotate the ball through the air
Strike runners	Attacking players who enter the line at pace to receive the ball
Sweepers	Players who hang back from the line (wall) of defence so that they can pick up any runners who penetrate it (usually the position adopted by the fullback)
Swerve	A change of a player's direction of run by arcing away from a defender
Switch	The transfer of the ball to a player who is running, to change the direction from which the ball has come
Tackle line	An imaginary line that is plotted mid-way between the attackers and defenders

INDEX

attack 3–4, 9–13, 18, 22–3

back row 38–43
   contact skills 39
   line-outs 42
   positional variations 43
   scrums 40–2
   tackling 39
back three 2–7
   attack/counter-attack 3–4
   defence 4–6
   positional variations 6–7
blind-side flanker, see back row

centres 8–15
   attack 9–13
   defence/tackling 13–14
   positional variations 14–15
contact 11–12
contact skills 39
continuity practice games 79–87
   beating the first defender using support 79–85
   contesting possession on the floor 86–7

defence 4–6, 13–14, 19, 23–4

fly-half 16–20
   attack 18
   defence 19
   handling 17
   kicking 19–20
   running and evasion 18
fullback, see back three

games for understanding 121–44
   4 v 2: 125–6
   attacking a drift defence 143–4
   counter-attack 139–40
   defensive line game 141–2
   Fijian touch 128–9
   five lives 132–3
   jailbreak 121–2
   line-out end ball 126–7
   numbers touch 129–30
   operating a drift defence 137–8
   organising back-line defence 135–6
   outside channel: wide passing 123–4
   Parramatta touch 130–1
   ruck and maul 134–5

handling 9–10, 17, 22
handling practice games 47–66
   2 v 1: 53–4
   3 v 2: 55–6
   catching a high ball 63–4
   general handling skills 61–2
   handling under pressure 49–50
   pass and move using scrum-half pass 59–60
   piggy in the middle 47
   receive and pass 51–2
   restarts: jumping to catch, supported 65–6
   standing scrum-half pass without back lift 57–8
   touch ground-pass 48–9
hooker 29–33
   line-outs 31–3
   scrums 30–1
hydration *xi*

inside centre, see centres

kicking 12, 19–20, 22
kicking practice games 88–96
   box kick 95–6
   drop kick 94–5
   grubber 90–1
   grubber kick goals 92–3
   punt 88–9
   rugby netball – kicking 89–90

left winger, see back three
line-out 27–8, 31–3, 36, 42
line-out practice games 113–18

line-out 117–18
line-out jumping: shadowing jumper 113–14
line-out supporting: introducing safe technique 114–15
line-out supporting: safe technique 116–17

mauling 39

number 8, *see* back row
nutrition *xi*

open play 28, 37
open-side flanker, *see* back row
outside centre, *see* centres

passing 9–10
principles of play *viii-ix*
prop forward 25–8
  line-outs 27–8
  open play 28
  restarts 28
  scrums 26–7

restarts 28, 37
right winger, *see* back three
rucking 39
running and evasion 10–11, 18, 22
running and evasion practice games 68–77
  change of pace, sidestep and swerve 70–1
  decision-making 74–7
  running lines 72–3

stuck in the mud 69
truck and trailer 68

scrum 26–7, 30–1, 35–6, 40–2
scrum-half 21–4
  attack 22–3
  defence 23–4
scrum practice games 104–11
  body management in scrum 106–7
  body shape in scrum 105–6
  power crawl and tyre push 104
  scrum 108–9
  scrummaging in units 110–11
second row 34–7
  line-outs 36
  open play 37
  restarts 37
  scrums 35–6

tackling 13–14, 39
tackling practice games 97–102
  repetitive tackle drill 101–2
  tackling 97–8
  turtle grid 99–100
throwing technique 32–3

warm-ups *x*
  jailbreak 121–2
  pass and move using scrum-half pass 59–60
  piggy in the middle 47
  stuck in the mud 69
  touch ground-pass 48–9
  truck and trailer 68
  turtle grid 99–100